RODIN
A BRILLIANT LIFE

1840
Birth of François-Auguste-René Rodin in Paris on 12 November

1854 14 YEARS
He started attending classes at the imperial school of drawing and mathematics, known as La Petite École.

1857
He left La Petite École and sought admission to the École des Beaux-Arts. He failed three times.

1858 18 YEARS
He worked for several sculptors, decorators, ornementalists and jewellers.

1862
Death of his sister Maria. Stricken by this loss, Rodin joined the Order of the Holy Sacrament for a few months.

1864 24 YEARS
Start of his collaboration with Carrier-Belleuse. He met Rose Beuret, aged 20 years, who became his life-long companion. Birth of Camille Claudel.

1865
The mask of the *Man with the Broken Nose* was turned down by the Salon des Artistes Français.

1866 26 YEARS
Birth of Auguste-Eugène Beuret, only son of Rodin, who he never recognised.

1867
He worked as a *praticien* (sculptor's assistant) for several ornementalists.

1870 30 YEARS
He enlisted in the army as a corporal in the Garde Nationale, but was discharged because of his shortsightedness.

1871
He joined Carrier-Belleuse in Belgium, where he spent 6 years.
Death of his mother.

1873 33 YEARS
He signed a partnership agreement with the Belgian sculptor Antoine-Joseph Van Rasbourgh.

1874
He participated in decorating the Palais des Académies in Brussels and painted a series of landscapes of the forest of Soignes.

1875 35 YEARS
A marble version of the *Man with the Broken Nose* was exhibited at the Salon. Study trip to Italy where he admired the work of Michelangelo.

1877
He exhibited *The Age of Bronze* at the Cercle Artistique et Littéraire of Brussels, then at the Salon in Paris. Rodin was accused of having cast his figure from life. He left Brussels for Paris and undertook his first tour of cathedrals.

1879 39 YEARS
He worked at the Manufacture de Sèvres until December 1882.

1880
He moved into his first studio in the marble depository at 182 rue de l'Université, which he kept until he died. The French State purchased *The Age of Bronze* and commissioned *The Gates of Hell* for the future Museum of Decorative Arts. He started to frequent artistic and literary salons.

1881 41 YEARS
The French State purchased a model of *Saint John the Baptist Preaching*. He learned engraving from his friend Legros in London.

1883
He met Camille Claudel who was 18 years old at the time. Death of his father. He made the *Bust of Victor Hugo*.

1885 45 YEARS
The city council of Calais commissioned a commemorative monument to Eustache de Saint Pierre, know later as the *Monument to the Burghers of Calais*.

1887
He was appointed knight of the Légion d'honneur. He illustrated a copy of "Les Fleurs du Mal" by Baudelaire belonging to Paul Gallimard.

1888 48 YEARS
The State ordered an enlarged marble version of *The Kiss* for the 1889 Universal Exhibition.
First exhibition of *The Thinker* (small-scale model) in Copenhagen.

1889
He was appointed a founding member of the Sociéte nationale des Beaux-Arts.
Commission for the *Monument to Claude Lorrain*, which was inaugurated in Nancy in 1892.
Joint exhibition with Claude Monet at the Georges Petit Gallery.
Co... *Monument to* ...he ...rst model of ...d down.

...olie ...los Payen, ...o meet ...ew statue of Victor Hugo, this time standing, for the Pantheon. The first project for the *Monument to Victor Hugo* was ordered for the Jardin du Luxembourg. The Société des Gens de Lettres commissioned a *Monument to Balzac*.

1892 52 YEARS
He was promoted Officer of the Légion d'Honneur.

1893
Rodin rented the Villa des Brillants in Meudon and hired Bourdelle as his *praticien*.

1895 55 YEARS
Inauguration in Calais of the *Monument to the Burghers of Calais*.

1896
Major exhibition with Puvis de Chavannes and Carrière in Geneva where photographs of Rodin's works were displayed for the first time.

1897 57 YEARS
Goupil published 142 heliographed drawings by Rodin, with a preface by Octave Mirbeau. The *Monument to Victor Hugo* was exhibited at the Salon de la Nationale.

1898
Break-up of his relationship with Camille Claudel. The Société des Gens de Lettres turned down the plaster version of the statue of *Balzac*, presented at the Salon of the Société Nationale des Beaux-Arts.

1899 59 YEARS
Commission for a *Monument to Puvis de Chavannes*. First monographic exhibition in Brussels, then Rotterdam, Amsterdam and The Hague. The large-scale version of *Eve* was exhibited at the Salon de la Nationale.

1900
Inauguration of the Rodin pavilion at Place de l'Alma in Paris, on the occasion of the Universal Exhibition. Creation of a Rodin Institute (Rodin was associated with Bourdelle and Desbois through an agreement).

1901 61 YEARS
The Rodin pavilion was dismantled, rebuilt in the garden in Meudon and converted into a studio. Major exhibition of photographs of Rodin's works by Eugène Druet at the Galerie des Artistes Modernes.

1902
Major Rodin exhibition in Prague. Successful tour of Moravia. He met the poet Rainer Maria Rilke who became his secretary in 1905.

1903 63 YEARS
He was appointed Commander of the Légion d'Honneur.

1905
He was appointed member of the Council of the Beaux-Arts, and awarded an honorary degree by the Université d'Iéna.

1906 66 YEARS
The Thinker was placed in front of the Pantheon. He executed a series of watercolours of the Cambodian dancers who had performed at the Colonial Exhibition in Marseilles. Meeting with the Japanese dancer Hanako. The drawings exhibited in Weimar caused an uproar.

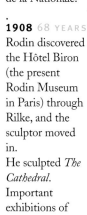

1907
First major exhibition devoted exclusively to his drawings at the Bernheim Jeune Gallery in Paris. *The Walking Man* (large-scale model) was exhibited at the Salon de la Nationale.

1908 68 YEARS
Rodin discovered the Hôtel Biron (the present Rodin Museum in Paris) through Rilke, and the sculptor moved in. He sculpted *The Cathedral*. Important exhibitions of drawings in Vienna, Leipzig and Paris.

1910
Exhibition of drawings, photographs by Steichen and *The Thinker* at the Photo Secession of New York. Rodin was nominated Grand Officer of the Légion d'Honneur.

1911 71 YEARS
Royal Exhibition of the Fine Arts in Berlin (William II refused to award Rodin the Order of Merit). The French State commissioned a *Bust of Puvis de Chavannes* for the Pantheon. Acquisition of the group *The Burghers of Calais* by England for the Westminster Gardens. "L'Art", Entretiens by Paul Gsell was published by Grasset.

1912
Exhibition of drawings at the Nouvelle Bibliothèque of Lyons. Inauguration of the Rodin Room in the Metropolitan Museum of New York.

1913 73 YEARS
Exhibition of Rodin's collection of antiques at the Faculty of Medicine in Paris. Camille Claudel was confined to a mental hospital.

1914
Publication of "Les Cathédrales de France", illustrated by one hundred facsimiles of drawings by Rodin, with a preface by Charles Morice. Rodin fled from the war and left for England with Rose. He stayed in Rome with the Marshall family.

1915 75 YEARS
Another trip to Rome. Rodin made a *Bust of Pope Benedict XV*.

1916
Rodin fell seriously ill. Three successive donations (1st April, 13 September and 25 October) of the Rodin collections to the State. The Chamber of Deputies, and then the Senate, accepted the donation, and the National Assembly voted for the establishment of a Rodin Museum in the Hôtel Biron.

1917 77 YEARS
29 January : Rodin married Rose Beuret in Meudon.
14 February : death of Rose
17 November : death of Rodin.
He was buried on 24 November in Meudon, next to Rose. Their tomb is dominated by *The Thinker*.

Rodin
A BRILLIANT LIFE

TOUT L'ŒUVRE • MARIE-PIERRE DELCLAUX

Front cover: Anonymous, *Portrait of Auguste Rodin wearing a jacket stained with plaster,* albumen paper, 1880, ph.311.

Back cover: *Notebooks of drawings by Auguste Rodin.*

Warning: Unless otherwise stated, the pieces of work and documents cited or reproduced are housed in the Rodin museum.

Published by the Éditions du musée Rodin

Editorial design, production and marketing : Edwige Ridel, Annie-Claude Demagny, Vincent Brocvielle & Julie Montaudon

Graphic design and layout : IP3
Photoengraving: Fotimprim
Printing : Imprimerie Chirat

Diffusion: musée Rodin
77, rue de Varenne 75007 Paris
servcom@musee-rodin.fr

DANGER
LE PHOTOCOPILLAGE
TUE LE LIVRE

RODIN
A BRILLIANT LIFE

"To open our eyes, we must know how to close them. An eye that is always open, always vigilant – the fantasy of Argus – becomes dry. A dry eye may perhaps see everything, all the time. But it will see badly. To see well, we need all our tears – a paradox of experience. […] We must open our eyes to be attentive, to respect the object of our historic questioning. But we must also know how to close our eyes to see the object better, to interpret it and understand how it affects us. We must accept the fluttering of our eyelids. That is when tears well up, while the visible emerges behind the flimsy drapery of our eyelids. To see well – including, and above all, **an object of time** *– we must know how to open but also close our eyes."*

(Didi-Huberman G., *Ninfa Moderna*, Paris, Gallimard, 2002, p. 127).

A sculptor with a flowing beard, a disparaged intruder who jostled retinas, known for his scandals, audacity and conquests, an extraordinary modeller attributed with a thousand intentions, this is Rodin. Solitary, above all. Engrossed in his work, body and soul. An unavoidable rock looming on the horizon at the turn of a period and a century.

He never talked much about himself. This is confirmed by his contemporaries. "[…] it is necessary to extricate the sentences one by one. And when he talks to you, it is with a soft, hesitant voice, repeating 'isn't that so?' every minute, like rings in a chain that he will use to link his ideas together; it does not flow naturally from its source. Do not ask him for picturesque details or anecdotes because he will not give them to you. 'What is the point', he would ask, 'Surely an artist worthy of that name is completely wrapped up in his work?'" [1]

Strangely enough, the mass of his personal archives is parsimonious. He discloses his life, drop by drop, from one incidental story to another. It is useless to hover over them to acquire an overall understanding. It is not a question of time. Years of rubbing shoulders with him will only release a few more facets of a completely self-absorbed personality, outside the boundaries of time and space, yet firmly anchored at the turning point of the 20th century. By focusing on his all-consuming work, there is a tendency to forget the man as he emerges, little by little. And this is what he himself would have wished, "less anecdotes and more ideas", as he put it. All he wanted to talk about was observation, study and work. And yet he has left us much more, and what used to be his present which he wished to conceal is now of interest to us.

[1] Jean-Bernard, "Lettre parisienne – Chez Rodin", *L'Express*, 22 May 1898.

LEFT PAGE
Léopold Reutlinger,
PORTRAIT OF RODIN WEARING A PINCE-NEZ,
albumen print, 1897, Ph.141.

Life is like a trajectory but Rodin's life was so closely tied to his work that it is impossible to relate it along the lines of a chronology without losing or forgetting the essential. It is therefore worth taking the risk of approaching his life through its multiple but not exhaustive – facets, of viewing his portrait through a kaleidoscope, under infinitely subjective angles. Just to see. By defocusing thought, the resulting image may give a fleeting glimpse of his personality so that it can be set aside in order to understand it through another facet. Such is the wealth and complexity of a man who is placed in the spotlight with all his contradictions, and it is perhaps the condition for understanding this sensitivity. There is no other intention.

Etienne Clémentel,
**RODIN GOING DOWN THE STEPS
OF THE HÔTEL BIRON,**
autochrome, 1915, Ph.6002.

Notebooks of drawings by Auguste Rodin.

I have not changed my life …

FAITHFUL

"This gentle appearance is one of the most striking features of the extraordinary physiognomy before you! […] . At first glance, the face itself seems to talk of peace and gentleness, built of straight and precisely fixed lines, with no violent clashes, well framed by healthy hair and a beard, blonde and long, in harmony with the complexion. But this beard is strong and powerfully attached, but the hair is thick. And although the eyes are blue, a tender blue, they are embedded under a prominent arcade, capable of containing lasting memories of forms perceived in nature. These light blue eyes are full of goodness, but they also shine proudly. And if the forehead seems to be of a great purity, the eyelids bear the weight of much research, marked by the bruises of laborious nights, endless days and constant fatigue."[1]

Nadar,
PORTRAIT OF RODIN WITH SHORT-CROPPED HAIR, WEARING A PINCE-NEZ, printing-out paper with mat collodion, 1891, Ph.176.

"Deep down inside him he had the obscurity, refuge and calm of a house, and he himself was the sky above, the surrounding forest, and the expanse, he was the river that flowed endlessly in front. […] He had hardened himself, rejecting the superfluous, and he stood out among other men, as if protected by an old bark."[2] Rainer Maria Rilke described Rodin as an intrinsic solidity, a man with deep roots, a permanence.

The fidelity of his heart and mind was outstanding, his gratitude fleeting yet persistent. It appeared to be directed at those who punctuated his success and served his work. To these people, he knew how to say thank you. Others, those in the wings, those who were able to accompany, encourage and support him, he did not talk about, for they were discarded or forgotten when he looked back on his life, they were left behind along the trajectory of his career.

First of all, there was his family, perhaps too closely associated in his mind to suffering and loss, exorcised in his work but leaving wounds that never healed. Those who allowed him, at the age of fourteen to take the path leading to La Petite École[3], who understood and respected his aspirations. His father, Jean-Baptiste,

LEFT PAGE

Haweis et Coles,
RODIN AND HIS DOGS IN MEUDON, silver gelatin print, 1904, Ph.1225.

Albert Harlingue,
RODIN IN HIS STUDIO IN MEUDON, NEAR A MONUMENTAL VERSION OF THE THINKER, gelatin silver print, 1906, Ph.10164.

Anonymous,
RODIN AS A CHILD ON HIS MOTHER'S LAP ? daguerreotype, Ph.2116.

[1] Maillard L., *Auguste Rodin statuaire*, Paris, H. Floury, 1899, pp. 23, 25.

[2] Rilke R.M., Letter to Lou Andreas-Salomé, Oberneuland, near Bremen, 8 August 1903; *Correspondance, Oeuvres 3*, Paris, Le Seuil, 1976, pp. 29-30.

[3] This was a school specialised in Drawing and Mathematics, the future Ecole des Arts Décoratifs, given this name to distinguish it from the Grande Ecole, in other words, the Ecole des Beaux-Arts. It trained craftsmen, decorators and ornamentalists.

1 - Jean-Baptiste Rodin,
LETTER TO HIS SON AUGUSTE,
circa 1860, Ma.179.

an employee of the Prefecture de Police, was always behind him during his periods of profound doubts. He inculcated him with fervour and courage, work and order, and gave his son invaluable encouragement and support *(fig. 1)*. His sister Maria, who was three years older, was his constant confidant. Her premature death carried away all her light-hearted conversations and confidence, freezing him permanently in discreet emotions and a silence that only sculpture could transcend *(fig. 2)*. These were important figures in his life, and they were loved, there is no doubt about that, for the notes he scribbled nearly sixty years later sometimes reveal traces of this constancy in his fleeting memories.

There were his friends, too few in number, the ones from his youth, like Léon Fourquet at La Petite École, with whom he shared so many books and the first

2 - Anonymous,
AUGUSTE RODIN AND HIS SISTER MARIA,
albumen print, circa 1859, Ph.2.

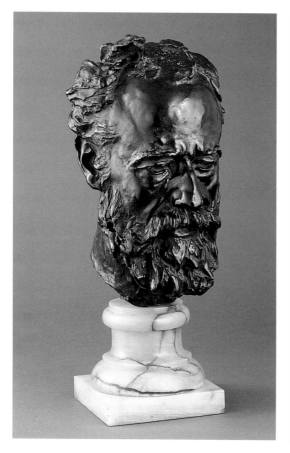

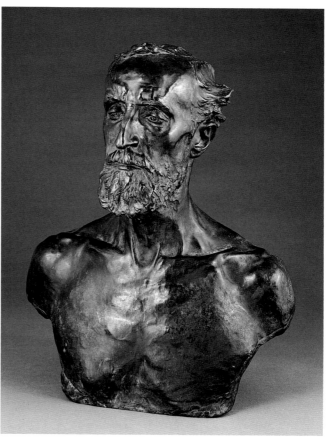

3 - Auguste Rodin,
ALPHONSE LEGROS,
bronze, 1881-1882, S.1060.

4 - Auguste Rodin,
JULES DALOU,
bronze, 1883, S.871.

emotional stirrings of art, in a spirit of emulation and simplicity that Rodin would never find again. He met Alphonse Legros *(fig. 3)* on the same school benches and would say of his drawings that they were "already by a master"[4]. He was the artist who taught him engraving in England in 1881. As for Jules Dalou, he remembered him as his "first friend" even though they actually met later[5] *(fig. 4)*.

And then there were those he did not hesitate to mention, the Belgian and French sculptors who were highly considered at that time and who actively helped him in 1877 to obtain recognition for his first big figure, *The Age of Bronze.* Among these artists were Falguière, Boucher and Chapu. They all supported him during the crucial period when he was trying desperately to be admitted to the official Salon circles, and seeking recognition for his years of hard labour. The numerous busts left by the sculptor are, in some cases, a kind of belated citation, a way of working while displaying his gratitude or affection. Doctor Thiriar and the chemist Van

4 Anonymous, "Alphonse Legros et Dijon", *Paris-Journal,* 5 June 1913.

5 "We met each other when we were very young, at an ornementalist who used to forget to pay us, so that we were obliged to leave him, Dalou and I: he to work for a taxidermist and I to work for another boss who was more punctual than the first one."

5 - Auguste Rodin,
ALBERT-ERNEST CARRIER-BELLEUSE,
patinated terracotta, 1882, S.1981.

Berkalaere who discreetly assisted him in Belgium during a period of financial
difficulty, earned their effigies in terracotta and in marble.

Others include the person who was responsible for the first to acknowledge his
talent, the painter Jean-Paul Laurens: "one of my oldest friends. [...] His affection
for me was always constant. It was he who obtained for me the commission for *The
Burghers of Calais*. [...] I am profoundly grateful to him for having pushed me into
creating one of my best works. It was a great pleasure to make his bust."[6]
And of course, there was Carrier-Belleuse, the widely known and acclaimed sculptor
of the Empire, who fashioned floral and beribboned busts that delighted his
bourgeois patrons so much *(fig. 5)*. Rodin worked for him for nearly twenty years.
First as a young decorator, then in Belgium during the 1871 war, and finally at the
Manufacture of Sèvres when he had become its Director. Rodin, who knew he was
indebted to him, admitted late in the day: "I owe much to Carrier-Belleuse who

(Coquiot G., *Rodin à l'Hôtel de
Biron et à Meudon*, Paris, Ollendorf,
1917, pp. 109-110).

6 Rodin A., *L'Art, entretiens réunis
par Paul Gsell*, Paris, Bernard
Grasset, 1911, p. 188.

taught me my craft." Even if he added: "Or rather, I used to owe much to him for he gave me a lot of advice, which I subsequently repaid."[7] It is thanks to him that Rodin learned how to reflect on different interpretations and variations of the same form, for Carrier-Belleuse had mastered this technique perfectly for commercial purposes. The art of multiplying would be echoed later in his research for simple forms of vases for the Manufacture *(fig. 6)*.

6 - Auguste Rodin,
SIX VASES,
graphite, ink patches, on ruled paper,
circa 1874 ? D.7630, f° 6 r°

Rodin asked for another name to be mentioned next to his in the official catalogue of the Salon des Artistes Français of 1875, for his first exhibition in France. This was the name of Barye listed, incorrectly, next to Carrier-Belleuse, as Rodin's teacher. It is true he had met him earlier at the Museum of Natural History but he only paid him a late – and somewhat immoderate – tribute, tinged with regret: "I was too foolish at that time to understand the genius of Barye and to be influenced by it. Much later, I acknowledged the place he occupies among our great sculptors, among the very best."[8] A big mistake committed in his youth, as he himself admitted[9], which no belated praise for the great sculptor could rectify, but which prompted Gustave Geffroy to say, "[…] although he was not actually a student of Barye, he has become so."[10]

Rodin only remembered one teacher. In 1913, having become famous, he had no hesitation in writing a posthumous tribute as a preamble in a publication on the method used by his master: "I have still retained most of what he taught me."[11] This teacher was Horace Lecoq de Boisbaudran, whose totally innovative teaching methods at La Petite École were based on exercising the memory by copying. In addition to the school curriculum, he trained some of his students to acquire a keen sense of observation[12] and sharpened their sensitivity to the fleeting nature of the models' movements by making them work outdoors. Rodin probably did not have an opportunity to follow those classes but it is certain that the memory exercises taught by Lecoq turned out to be one of his most precious assets.

This training is reflected in the *Bust of Victor Hugo* of 1883. He related on numerous occasions how difficult it was to make it, referring to the name of his exceptional teacher who had given him the means to accomplish this technical feat. Victor Hugo refused to pose and only "tolerated (me) on the veranda of his home on condition

7 Rodin, quoted by Sacha Guitry, " Un film étonnant ", *Les Nouvelles,* 23 November 1939.

8 Fuss-Amore G., " Mes souvenirs parisiens: Auguste Rodin", *La Revue Belge,* 15 July 1929, p. 178.

9 Bourdelle E.-A., *La sculpture de Rodin,* Paris, Emile-Paul Frères, 1939, p. 27.

10 Geffroy G., "Le statuaire Rodin", *Les lettres et les arts,* September 1889, p. 292.

11 Lecoq de Boisbaudran H., *L'éducation de la mémoire pittoresque,* Paris, Henri Laurens, 1913.

12 "[He made me] draw a lot from memory and thus taught me how to observe; this has always been useful to me." "I made rapid progress after copied models, according to the methods of the time, many of which dated back to the foundation of the School. I recall having copied red chalk drawings after Boucher." (Dujardin-Beaumetz H., *Entretiens avec Rodin,* Paris, Paul Dupont, 1913, pp. 109-111).

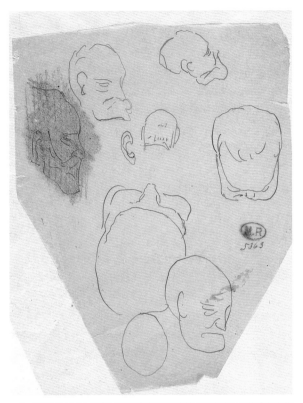

7 - Auguste Rodin,
STUDIES FOR THE HEAD OF VICTOR HUGO,
pen, ink and graphite on paper, 1883,
D.5363.

8 Anonymous,
BUST OF VICTOR HUGO IN CLAY
WITH RODIN IN THE BACKGROUND,
albumen print, 1883, Ph.353.

9 - John Marshall,
**RODIN IN ROME, ON THE TERRACE
OF JOHN MARSHALL'S,
LOOKING AT THE DOME OF ST PETER'S,**
gelatin silver print, December 1914,
Ph.10070.

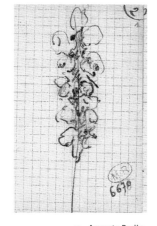

10 - Auguste Rodin,
SNAPDRAGON STEM,
pencil on a notebook page, 1913-1914 ?
D.6670, notebook 33, f°1 r°.

that I did not demand anything, contented myself with catching a glimpse of him briefly and immediately noting a few essential features"[13] *(figs. 7 and 8)*. He was therefore able to successfully fulfil his dream of capturing the features of the author who was the centre of attraction at the time and whose *Contemplations* had accompanied him since his early youth. This gave him an opportunity to finally silence accusations of casting from life, first made in 1877 in the case of *The Age of Bronze* and again in 1881 with reference to *Saint John the Baptist*. These accusations were never completely refuted but the fact that the famous Victor Hugo was unlikely to accept being cast from life was the best guarantee of Rodin's artistic integrity.

However, in his old age, within the obscurity of himself, Rodin finally took the time to return to his memories, and in addition to the gratitude expressed to those who helped him build up his career, a sense of relationship occasionally appears in his notebooks. The emotions of his early childhood surged before the memory of places, in an indescribable attachment to his feelings about the first whims of fate that led him to decide, at the age of fourteen, to be a sculptor.

An acute awareness of certain elements can be detected during his childhood. These leitmotifs would follow him throughout his life like punctuation: architecture, botany, and a little later, the 18th century, all associated with the names of people who were close to him and had backed him in discreet silence.[14] First of all, came his city, Paris, and with it the sky of the Ile de France. Michel Georges-Michel came across him contemplating this sky on the esplanade of the Invalides on 20 November 1913, and dreaming of sculpting it: "No other country in the world other than the Ile-de-France, not even Rome or Florence, has the softness of this sky."[15] Architecture also set the rhythm of his Parisian childhood and this was the reason for his sudden trip to Italy late in his life, around 1915 *(fig. 9)*. First of all, he grew

[13] Coquiot G., *op.cit.,* 1917, p. 106.

[14] "These old layers of my life, the foundation, my youth which was the point, the spear that carried the rest. Springing out of the roots of my parents, everything took me far away, and now the memory of them is like a religion for me and soon I too will become a memory." (Notebook n° 91, f°5 v° and 6 r°, Rodin Museum).

[15] Georges-Michel M., "Nos échos", *Le siècle,* 19 November 1908, p. 77.

under the shadow of the Val de Grâce, "rue des Fossés St. Jacques at the other end of my life, almost the first view I had then was the Val de Grâce – today St. Peter's [...] the kindness of my parents who allowed me to study until I was 17 years old [...] in their modest apartment on the 4th floor [...] I could see the diminutive neighbourhoods of Rome." [16] Later came Notre Dame, Saint-Eustache and all those districts of Paris where he loved to walk with Rose, his companion, to rediscover the beauty of his roots. It was this feeling of pride that gripped when contemplating the "Paris of Jean-Jacques Rousseau." [17]

And then further away, the French provinces and hidden churches with their well-preserved architecture beckoned to him [18]. Rodin escaped regularly to make short pilgrimages to cathedrals [19]. This breath of fresh air became vital during a period when Paris was undergoing the turmoil of restructuring. On one of those days, between 1906 and 1913, finding himself in front of the cathedral of Beauvais, which he knew well, having spent three years in the shadow of its buttresses when he was eleven years old, his emotions turned out to be intact. "I relive my childhood: the delightful garden where I used to take refuge to daydream; my eager joy in front of the jubilation of Cathedrals projecting their bell towers of pure shade, the freedom of a young man released into an intoxicating happiness [...] these impetuous moments flee like leaves falling from a tree" [20].

His memories are still very vivid about the ultimate attempt at schooling at an establishment run by Hippolyte, his paternal uncle, where he seemingly made no further progress. Spelling and arithmetic remained at elementary levels, perhaps because of an undetected myopia [21]. Recalling those three years, the young Rodin admitted in 1889 that he spent most of his time "in drawing fanciful designs, telling stories, and reciting imaginary descriptions to his comrades" [22]. However, this was of no importance because his uncle Hippolyte, who had a passion for French literature [23]

11 - Auguste Rodin,
MAPLE LEAF ?
pencil on a notebook page, 1913-1914 ?
D.6686, notebook 33, f° 17v°.

12 - Auguste Rodin,
ACANTHUS LEAF ?
pencil on a notebook page, 1913-1914 ?
D.6698, notebook 33, f° 28v°.

16 Notebook n° 11, f°10 v°, 11 r° and 12r°, around 1915 ?, Rodin Museum.

17 Cladel J., "Rodin et l'art gothique", *La Revue hebdomadaire*, 7 November 1908, p. 77.

18 "[...] there are marvellous sites, admirable monuments in our country [...] Despite pressing needs, I need to escape to immerse myself once again in these beneficial sources; there is no need to cross mountains and the sea, we have treasures in our own country." (Rodin A., *Le Gaulois*, 21 August 1903).

19 "Rodin, the sculptor, sometimes disappears from home for a few days without us knowing where he

goes, and when he returns and we ask him where he has been, he replies 'I have just been to see cathedrals'". (Goncourt E. and J., *Journal*, 14 June 1888, Paris, Robert Laffont, Bouquins coll., volume 3, p. 135).

20 Notes and Drafts, Xb-15, Rodin Museum.

21 "I could not see the figures on the blackboard. I have always been near sighted. As a child I did not know what was the matter and I hated mathematics because I could not see." (Cheruy R., "Rodin's Gate of Hell comes to America", *New York Herald Tribune*, 20 January 1929, p. 17). "The pupils followed Latin classes. I don't know why, but I never liked doing Latin, and I have

often regretted it; it may have changed my destiny." (Dujardin-Beaumetz H., *op. cit.*, 1913, p. 111).

22 Bartlett T.H., "Auguste Rodin sculptor", *The American Architect and Building News*, 19 January 1889, p. 27.

23 "He always felt grateful to this uncle [...] who he said had the mentality of a certain culture, admiring poets and old French authors." (Bénédite L., *Rodin*, Paris, Rieder F. & Cie., 1926, p. 7).

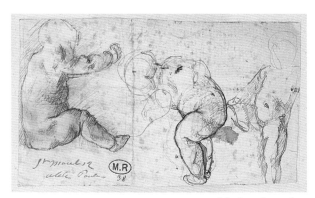

13 - Auguste Rodin,
THREE NAKED CHILDREN,
graphite and ink on buff paper,
circa 1870 ? D.38.

14 - Victor Pannelier,
BUST OF MME ROLL IN PLASTER AND CLAY,
IN THE STUDIO,
albumen print, Ph.314.

and "always sought in (his) teaching to inspire a taste for botany, (his) favourite science" [24] probably influenced his nephew's immoderate taste for reading and studying natural structures *(figs. 10 to 12)*. When he was nearly seventy years old, Rodin remembered his appreciation of flowers, even before he initiated his studies: "just as in my youth, my childhood, the box of flowers gave us small pleasures, now the whole garden gives me great pleasures" [25]. "It is amazing how a nasturtium can move me. In the flower box on the third floor, it climbed up to my parents' apartment: a pure soul in its place, the resignation of this nasturtium, so capricious in its flowering, so regularly flat in its leaves." [26] During those three decisive years, he developed an inner world, solitary activities and a fertile imagination that, along with his interest in history, reading and nature, intensified the wonder he felt for the Gothic style. He retained from his childhood spent "far away from luxury" [27], a great simplicity that could appear to be a little earthy to some people. "Obviously, I no longer wait for the omnibus, as in the past; but for the rest, I have not changed my life. Money has come too late; and we, at least a few artists like me, are unable to get used to its power." [28] Despite the money he started to earn, Rodin continued to enjoy the simple meals he ate since his childhood. [29] In 1894, the journalist Séverine observed with amusement that despite the frock coat and watch chain, "both opulent, perfect and marked by the rosette of the Légion d'Honneur. […] a gracefulness – if this term can be applied to men – upsets the harmony of this regularity: the spiciness of a flavour that is not so much bohemian as plebeian and earthy. It is nothing at all: just a minor discomfort in the shoulders, an irritable and disdainful gesture for anything that cramps or restrains him: a horror for overdressing that is inflicted on him – and with such loathing!" [30] Rodin, too absolute, gave himself away.

He became aware of 18th century art in a natural manner through the studies he undertook after leaving Beauvais. "La Petite Ecole had kept a few traces of 18th century education; life, feelings and grace were not banished; this can be seen clearly in my drawings"[31] *(fig. 13)*. With time, this "18th century education"[32] continued with Carrier-Belleuse, was transformed into a deep admiration when he understand its basic principles[33] *(fig. 14)*. This was the reason behind the invitation he received in 1908 from the poet Rainer Maria Rilke, who was his secretary for a while, to

24 Rodin Hippolyte, *Les plantes médicinales et usuelles …*, Paris, 1872, p. 1; *cf.* Grunfeld F.V., *Rodin*, Fayard, 1988, p. 22.

25 Notebook n° 74, f°41 r°, s.d., Rodin Museum.

26 Notebook n° 94, f°6 v°, after 1908, Rodin Museum.

27 Notebook n° 58, f°23 r°, between 1900 and 1914, Rodin Museum.

28 Coquiot G., *op. cit.*, 1917, p. 97.

29 For details about the food Rodin ate, see Vassalo I., *Rodin, Le festin d'une vie*, Paris, Le Chêne, 1997.

30 Séverine, "Auguste Rodin", *Le Journal*, 10 November 1894. He himself noted, "Just as the gown is necessary to walk about and think, trousers remind you of the shame of being so badly built." (Notes and Drafts, VI-Df, taken from Notebook n° 59, f°20 v°, Rodin Museum).

31 Dujardin-Beaumetz H., *op.cit.*, 1913, p. 112.

32 "I received the education of the 18th century." (Cladel J., *Rodin, sa vie glorieuse, sa vie inconnue*, Paris, Grasset, 1936, p. 72).

33 Coquiot G., *Le vrai Rodin*, Paris, Jules Tallandier, 1913, pp. 221-222.

15 - Etienne Clémentel,
Rodin on the steps of the Hôtel Biron,
autochrome, circa 1915, Ph.6003.

16 - Cl. Lémery,
RODIN IN A ROOM ON THE GROUND FLOOR
OF THE HÔTEL BIRON,
aristotype, 22 April 1912, Ph.196.

17 - Anonymous
RUINS OF THE FORMER CHÂTEAU D'ISSY,
DESTROYED IN 1870,
postcard, before 1907, Ph.1283.

visit the Hôtel Biron where he lived with about fifty other tenants[34]. He knew perfectly well that Rodin would not resist the slightly outmoded charm of the mansion designed by Jean Aubert in 1728, and its abandoned garden, a stone's throw from the Invalides *(fig. 15)*. Unsurprisingly, Rodin immediately moved into four rooms on the ground floor *(fig. 16)*. Gradually, he took possession of the entire mansion, and from 1911 onwards was its sole occupant. The prestigious Hôtel Biron found its echo in the façade of the château of Issy, also dating back to the 18th century, which was burnt down under the Commune. Between 1907 and 1910, the sculptor had it rebuilt in his garden in Meudon, "like a Greek temple", underlined the press *(figs. 17 and 18)*. He turned the two settings of his public and private life into a two-headed museum by making three successive donations to the State, to bring together permanently his sculptures, as well as his collections and samples of the architecture of the century that stirred his first feelings as an artist.

18 - Albert Harlingue,
Rodin in front of the façade of the Château d'Issy in Meudon,
printing-out paper, after 1908, Ph.6.

34 Including Jean Cocteau, Isadora Duncan and Henri Matisse.

learning to open one's eyes ...

AVID

"His short sighted eyes, usually sheltered behind a pince-nez, blinked a little, as if they wanted to discern the whole rather than the details. They were very sensitive and frequently red. Sometimes, they opened immensely, disclosing very limpid pupils that seemed to want to absorb the universe. His thick beard, which had turned white after being red, accentuated the faun-like aspect of his profile with its big, straight nose prolonging the line of his forehead. Rodin was short, with a broad chest. Intermittently, slight quivers ran through his arms and shoulders, as if he were charged with electricity. I mention this because it leads one to suppose that genius is partly due to an exceptional nervous tension." [1]

Albert Harlingue,
PORTRAIT OF RODIN, DISHEVELLED, AT THE HÔTEL BIRON,
gelatin silver print, 1906, Ph.749.

An amazing compulsion, a voracious appetite, and a deep-rooted need to ingest the visible in quantities and continuously lay at the junction of Rodin's extraordinarily powerful work and his interest for the world surrounding him, participating in both at the same time. Paradoxically, although he was a gourmet in his appreciation of the world and its tiniest subtleties, he was nevertheless and, above all, greedy. Was it the hardships of his youth that justified his constant need to nourish himself without restraint of all that was set before his eyes, to take advantage avidly of the simplest pleasures? [2] Being a mediocre student but a determined and obstinate one, only diligent work combined by this incredible capacity to absorb could enable him to attain his goals. Did his parallel interest for drawing leave him any choice? The young Rodin wanted to learn everything, and no amount of studying could satisfy his appetite. So for him, everything served as a lesson.

Very soon, by the end of his six-year stay in Belgium in 1877, nature had already become his unique reference. This is where he really discovered it, in the course of his walks through the forest of Soignes and the woods of La Cambre [3]. He told Bartlett, his biographer, that he "went everywhere in Belgium, walking end of miles, and saw everything." [4] The notebooks he later stuffed deep into his pocket recorded his spiralling reflections on natural structures in a jerky handwriting. In the calm of the early morning, as soon as he got out of bed, he found material in the garden

LEFT PAGE

Auguste Rodin,
LANDSCAPE IN BELGIUM ?
red chalk drawing on beige paper, between 1871 and 1877 ? D.7.

Auguste Rodin,
SCENE OF AN INTERIOR AFTER THE BACK COURTYARD OF A DUTCH HOUSE BY PIETER DE HOOCH (PARIS, THE LOUVRE, INV. 1372),
graphite, pen and blue ink wash on squared buff paper, before 1870 ? D.48.

Auguste Rodin,
STILL LIFE,
Graphite and watercolour on pasted buff paper, before 1870 ? D.103.

Auguste Rodin,
THREE COWS RECLINING,
graphite on a notebook, D.6220 and 6221, notebook 4, f°5 v°.

[1] Gsell P., "Souvenirs sur Rodin", *L'Illustration*, 9 November 1940, pp. 242-243.

[2] "It is so pleasant in the morning; it is only the poor who are familiar with mornings." (Notebook n° 47, 1st inside cover, around 1912? Rodin Museum.

[3] "It is over there that I started to look at the world with my eyes, to love Nature deeply, to discern and savour its nuances and to realise that one has but to look, to feel and to give back in order to make beauty." (Meunier M., "Rodin dans son art et dans sa vie", *Les Marges*, 15 April 1914, p. 249).

[4] Notes by Bartlett, Harvard University, Houghton.

to nourish his work[5]. It was a return to basics for annotations on simple references to geometry, structures and vegetal compositions. Rodin was always on the alert, describing in a notebook the straight line of a cedar branch like the stretched arm of *Victor Hugo,* or the interplay of shadows produced by the veins of a cabbage leaf. "… There is no doubt about it, I am merely an unsuccessful botanist. I can nevertheless understand, in my own way […] I study, leaning over the flowers along my path. What curious, different and countless expressions are at the disposal of an artist!"[6] Because the architecture of the cathedrals he admired so much was born of this nature, because it offered extraordinary structures for those who took the trouble to look, he never tired of its teaching and bowed before it[7]. Since Nature was perfect, it continued to be his model. And as he advanced in age and his strength failed him, it became his means of escape. In the end, his notes overlap each other in his notebooks. Will he only have enough time to draw conclusions? "How many times he was heard repeating this until the end of his life! […] Seeing … seeing … and understanding."[8] Rodin always wanted to know more, and inevitably he had to admit he would never finish learning[9]. As it is, he needed nearly thirty years to completely assimilate the teaching of men, and to integrate himself into this tradition[10]. He always had an unquenchable thirst for the visible.

"As a child, as far back as I can remember, I used to draw. A grocer, whose shop my mother went to, used to wrap prunes in bags made of pages from illustrated books, and even engravings. I would copy them. They were my first models", he recalled[11]. These first – anonymous – masters would be joined by the great ancient Greeks whose sculptures he studied at the Louvre, Michelangelo, the "last of the Gothics", his teacher Lecoq de Boisbaudran, and his employer for several years, Carrier-Belleuse. He learned from all of them, and they all helped him to advance. From the last two, he acquired the techniques required to become the perfect

5 "I have only to open my eyes and look in front of me not to feel bored. The beauty of plants is so complex, so opulent that one always discovers a particle, and it is always new." (Rodin, quoted by Canudo R., "Une visite à Rodin", *La Revue hebdomadaire,* 5 April 1913, p. 26).

6 Rodin A., *Les Cathédrales de France,* Paris, Albin Michel, 1914, p. 126.

7 "In seeing all that surrounds me, that I admire without understanding, I can well admit that somewhere above me there is a spirit that willed all this Nature, which I adore". (Cladel J., *Auguste Rodin pris sur la vie,* Paris, La Plume, 1903, p. 101).

8 Jeanès J.E.S., *D'après nature, Souvenirs et portraits,* Besançon, Granvelle, 1946, p. 124.

9 "In his hand, lying on a damp cloth, he held a small torso in clay that he tapped with a roughing-chisel. […] 'I give up trying to understand what sculpture is … This awful little torso does not want to know anything about it … Look at it! It's round, it's lifeless, it doesn't capture light … It is aggravating to grow old … and to say to yourself that you won't succeed.'" (Jeanès J.E.S., *op.cit.,* pp. 153-154).

10 "I studied antiques, the sculpture of the Middle Ages, and I returned to healthy and comforting nature. I hesitated at the beginning, then I grew bolder as I started to feel I was in the genuine tradition of truth and freedom. It is I who is in the tradition – the École des Beaux-Arts broke away from it eighty years ago – I am in the tradition of the Primitives, the Egyptians, the Greeks, the Romans. I simply applied myself to copying nature." (Rodin, quoted by Claris E., "L'impressionnisme en sculpture", *La Nouvelle Revue,* 1st June 1901, p. 327).

11 Dujardin-Beaumetz H., *op.cit.,* 1913, p. 111.

craftsman he strove to be, and from the others he received lessons on how to become an artist.

When he started attending La Petite École in 1854, he probably had a presentiment that drawing would be his last resort. In any event, he used it as a means to understand, note, identify and collect forms. For him, drawing was the tool he needed to accomplish his ambitions, it was the only way to succeed. Lecoq de Boisbaudran spent a year sharpening his eye to grasp every detail. This turned out to be a precious lesson when, nearly twenty years later in Belgium, Rodin, dazzled by Rubens, felt the need to fix him in his memory. "Rubens, over there in Belgium, is an obsession. He pervades your entire body. So I tried to reproduce the *Christ Pierced with a Spear;* when I couldn't remember the tones, I jumped on the tram and went to the museum to look at it again, and then I came back home to do them …" [12] *(fig. 19)* This was an education for his eyes and his hands, and already the first signs of this complementarity took shape in his writing and drawing, in the notes that constantly filled up dozens of notebook many years later.

19 - Auguste Rodin,
Copy after « Christ Pierced by a Spear » by Rubens,
oil on paper pasted on canvas,
between 1871 and 1877, P.7244.

The following year, during modelling classes, he learned to work by copying antique sculptures, with the "admiration of feeling that one can draw from far and without copying a drawing. The admiration of knowing that there are young people who make antique figures with clay. I already know how to draw, but I immediately understand when an older student tells me about how to bring out the contrasts of a figure. By the end of a week, I understood and the rest was merely development in sculpture." [13] He seemed to recall – erroneously – that the great Carpeaux showed up from time to time[14]. This confusion was probably due to the immense admiration he felt for him,

12 Anonymous, "Une peinture de Rodin", *France et Allemagne,* 18 May 1913. It seems that Rodin did indeed paint many pictures after Rubens from memory, if one is to believe Bartlett's notes: "In love with Rubens, I painted from many of the pictures I saw there in my room". (Harvard University, Houghton).

13 Rodin, notes to Gaston Schéfer, Institute Library, Paris. Bartlett points out that Rodin only reproduced "the more prominent portions and thinking that these ought to be some details to fill up the spaces, thus giving completer interest to his work, he put in such additional forms as he thought best." His myopia was discovered, "a fact wich no one had previously found out, although Auguste had often wondered why he did not see things as other boys did." (Bartlett T.H., *op. cit.,* 19 January 1889, p.28)

14 "In actual fact, he did not come often; but – I don't know why, for we were too young to understand it – we felt an instinctive admiration for him; one could say that we had a presentiment that he would become great man; […] later, after having seen his works, I looked at him only." (Dujardin-Beaumetz H., *op. cit.,* 1913, p. 101). Carpeaux had in fact already left the School where he had been a tutor from 1851 to 1854. Rodin could only have crossed his path in 1854.

combined with a desire to find a mentor, because, it must be admitted, he was a little disoriented. Already at this stage, he was incapable of restricting himself to what he was taught and constantly sought to assimilate the maximum in a minimum of time. He wanted to acquire freedom through the tools. And drawing was his strength [15].

There was no time to lose. To analyse, he needed to learn how to observe. Rilke, who met him in September 1902 to write his biography, described him as being totally absorbed by his studies. "One moment he is like a schoolboy, a beginner, an observer and imitator of lost beauties that until now have lain among dormant, distracted or indifferent beings. Another moment, he is attentive, with nothing escaping his eye, a lover constantly receiving, a person of patience who does not ration his time nor dreams of obtaining an immediate advantage. What he looks at, what he enfolds in his contemplation, is always, in his view, a unique universe where everything can happen" [16]. Objects-subjects, objects-thoughts, objects-ideas, objects-forms whose accumulation, before being physical, is entirely virtual, took shape through snatches of notes and drawings, which he appropriated in the strongest manner possible, by using a simple pencil [17]. "In the Louvre, a long time ago, the Olympian gods told me, like saints speaking to a monk in a cloister, all that a young man could usefully hear" [18]; "How many times I came here in the past, when I was barely fifteen years old. At first, I had a violent desire to become a painter. Colour attracted me. I often went up there to admire the Titians and Rembrandts. But, alas! I did not have enough money to buy canvasses and tubes of colour. To copy the Antiques, on the other hand, all I needed was paper and pencils. I was therefore obliged to work in the lower rooms only but soon I developed such a passion for sculpture that I no longer thought of anything else" [19]. His first passion was for Greece, and his first sketches and notes, already found an echo in 1855 in the studies he pursued at the same time in the Engravings Department of the Imperial Library. In view of his modest appearance, he had to content himself with the books left lying on the tables. "I had an avid spirit, everything was permitted." [20]

He was still avid enough to enrol in the free courses on literature and history

[15] "A man who has studied nature a lot, sees correctly, and has a quick mind. He can do, undo, reconstruct his work, analyse it, add to it, recompose it. But to be able to achieve this, as always in art, one must have drawn a lot. Drawing is a perpetual comparison. Someone who is incapable of establishing a figure exactly does not have the possibility of making variations."

(Dujardin-Beaumetz H., *op. cit.*, 1913, p. 76).

[16] Rilke R.M., letter to Lou Andreas-Salomé, Oberneuland, near Bremen, 8 August 1903, in *Correspondance, Oeuvres 3*, Paris, Le Seuil, 1976, p. 30.

[17] "Memories of my youth when, being unable to enter here or there

free, I nevertheless carried away with me millions of thoughts." (Coquiot G., *op. cit.*, 1917, p. 79).

[18] Rodin A., "A la Venus de Milo", *Rodin, sa vie, son oeuvre*, Paris, L'Art et les Artistes, 1914, p. 94.

organised by the City of Paris. At the Collège de France, he discovered Hugo, Musset, Lamartine, Dante, Virgil and Homer. With hindsight, he admitted much later that at the time he was striving "through lengthy reading to create [his own] aesthetics. Now, I realise that aesthetics is acquired through experience. […] Understanding is a slow and difficult process." [21]

He also attended Les Gobelins for drawing classes from five to eight in the evening to make up for the lack of classes on drawing from a live model at La Petite École. "We worked from a live model three hours on end, which meant eighteen hours a week. At the École des Beaux-Arts, they only worked for two hours, that is to say, twelve hours for one study, which was not enough. At Les Gobelins, they had remained faithful to the traditions of the 18th century; the drawing were more "in the round". An artist, M. Lucas, taught there without prejudice, which was rare at the time." [22]

20 - Auguste Rodin,
SKINNED SKELETON OF A HORSE'S LEGS,
graphite and ink on buff paper,
before 1870 ? D.236.

With the early retirement of his father in 1861, due to health reasons, the modest annual income of 1,550 francs was reduced even further. [23] Although Rodin had to work to help his family, he did not abandon his apprenticeship. While studying from live models, he familiarised himself with the anatomy of animals, first of all through books *(fig. 20)* and, not far from there, "at the Jardin des Plantes where Barye taught; I became friendly with his son. We were ill at ease among the amateurs and women, and I think we felt intimidated by the waxed parquet floors of the Library where the classes were held." They sought refuge in an uncomfortable

19 Rodin A., *op. cit.,* 1911, p. 274; Rodin did not obtain permission to copy paintings in the Louvre until 1862, six years after the date indicated on his admission card.

20 Dujardin-Beaumetz H., *op. cit.,* 1913, p. 112.

21 Rodin A., "Réflexions sur la beauté", *L'Opinion,* 11 June 1910.

22 Dujardin-Beaumetz H., *loc.cit.* Abel Lucas, painter and tapestry-maker, had been a teacher at Les Gobelins since 1848.

23 At that time, the minimum income to feed a family of four was estimated at 1,900 francs a year.

21 - Auguste Rodin,
SHEETS OF STUDIES,
graphite and ink on paper cut out and
pasted on cardboard,
between 1875 and 1877, D.205 to 221.

basement to copy "bits of animals, lions' paws" picked up from the amphitheatres.[24] However, he soon dropped these initial studies in anatomy to work on the morphology of animals directly from life, at the horse market in the district near Saint Marcel, and then from 1864 onwards, at the zoo in the Jardin des Plantes.

During his first trip to Italy at the end of 1875, Rodin also concentrated on the keen observation of Michelangelo, working on small pieces of paper [25]. Once again, there was only one technique: "After looking at these figures long and well I returned to my room at the hotel and began making sketches to test the depth of my own capacity of composition and of the impressions I had received."[26] On his return to Belgium, these small sketches, accumulated during the weeks of his first visit to Italy, found their place in his albums, juxtaposed by collage, without any real concern for arranging them in any particular order. Once these memories and impressions, food for thought and for study, were grouped together and captured in drawings, they could then be used for further reflection and would sometimes take shape with a touch of ink or gouache *(fig. 21)*. Ideas were fixed by visualising the whole, always

24 Dujardin-Beaumetz H., *op.cit.*, 1913, p. 113.

25 "When I went to Italy, having my head full of the Greek models I had studied passionately at the Louvre, I was very disconcerted by Michelangelo. In every way, he contradicted the truths that I thought I had permanently acquired. That is curious, I would say to myself, why is the torso curved this way, why is this hip lifted up and this shoulder lowered? I was very perturbed. And yet

through the detail, the corpus through the component, to transform it into a synthesis. All of these sheets of memories from Italy already bore traces of what would later become a mode of functioning: multiplying, assembling and exploiting.[27]

Not content with amassing over time, he amassed over space, as soon as this was feasible. Rodin was finally able to give free reign to his passion for collecting when he settled in the Villa des Brillants in Meudon in 1893. "[…] you open a door, and plaster ghosts appear; next to rabbit hutches, a kind of warehouse has become an Egyptian museum, with a collection of pieces of bronze, glass, fragments of figurines, the debris of antiquity, treasures discovered in bins along the quays, in junk shops, and Rodin would be filled with enthusiasm over one of these specimens, of no interest to the ordinary man, he would get carried away, he would go into raptures and praise antique art, the harmony of the curves, the perfect mastery of the lines."[28] Here too, these objects were collected to nourish a reflection without respite *(figs. 22 and 23)*. This is why he only occasionally added the paintings given to him by his painter friends, as these were usually relegated to the upper floors, and the few canvasses on the ground floor could be conjured away behind a curtain[29]. Rodin could not stop himself from buying[30], sometimes by entire lots, merely for the expressive quality of objects. He did not bargain and even though he was suspicious by nature, it appears that some dealers took advantage of his extravagance. There were few really good pieces in this collection, clearly pointing to an

22 - Anonymous,
A DISPLAY-CASE CONTAINING ANTIQUE MARBLES AT THE HÔTEL BIRON,
between 1912 and 1916, in Coquiot G., *Rodin à l' hôtel biron et à Meudon*, Paris, Ollendorf, 1917.

23 - Frank Bal,
RODIN SEATED IN THE MIDST OF HIS COLLECTION,
gelatin silver print, circa 1905, Ph.7004.

Michelangelo could not have been mistaken! I had to understand. I applied myself and succeeded." (Rodin A., *op. cit.*, 1911, p. 267).

26 Bartlett T.H., *op. cit.*, 9 February 1889, p. 65.

27 For information about the Rodin collection, see Garnier B., *Rodin, Antiquity is my youth*, Paris, Rodin Museum Publications, 2002.

28 Guillemot M., "Au Val Meudon", *Le Journal*, 17 August 1898.

29 *idem.*

30 "It is true that this passion puts a great strain on my budget." (Rodin, quoted by Gsell P., "Propos d'Auguste Rodin sur l'art et les artistes", *La Revue*, 1st November 1907, p. 100).

opportunistic behaviour for the sake of acquisition rather than a genuine passion. And thus, the sculptor sought to stimulate personal research through his feelings, with an obsession that was almost pathological.

Possessing to assimilate. Was that the condition? And how many objects did he really choose, observe and study them for their own sake? In the case of Rodin, the act of collecting implied having forms similar to what nature offered him at his immediate disposal. He himself admitted it again in 1910. "[…] it is important to learn to open your eyes. It is difficult." [31] It is clear he was still in the process of learning during that year. This is why he liked to surround himself with an accumulation of objects of all kinds and all qualities. In addition, it gave him the pleasure of sometimes taking the time to have another look at what "for me have a familiar enchantment. These plasters, these marbles, give me small lectures, they remind me of my pilgrimages to all the Cathedrals of France. What rapture! I hear vague modulations, followed by more distinct words and imperious stanzas. The souls of the Masters teach, they correct mine." [32] Accumulating for a better understanding was a way of putting this deaf dialogue into the plural instead of the singular, and it allowed a law, a principle, to become a lesson, to emerge from the mass. "Yes, one single law, everywhere the same harmony. A general spirit gives unity to all these works. […] Entering the truth, returning to nature, going back to principles: linking the present to the past." [33] "I returned wholeheartedly into the spirit of these plasters ten days ago when I was feeling sickly, I will join them, they have been there for years." [34] Thanks to the proliferation, by casting, of his own plasters, and their permanent contrast with his collection in the villa in Meudon, Rodin continued his efforts to understand conclusively. This collector of forms had a titanic memory, and he worked in silence, comparing objects in contemplation and meditation. The multitude remained permanently linked to his solitary work [35] in an incredible assembly *(fig. 24)*. In his view, the mass only existed through the elements composing it: "The detail is like blood circulating through the organism; it must be included in the whole, that envelops it but does not kill it. This is true simplification; this is what great artists strive to attain; it is a need." [36]

[31] Rodin A., "Rodin par lui-même", *Je sais tout,* 15 March 1910, p. 207.

[32] Rodin A., *op. cit.,* 1914, p. 48.

[33] Rodin A., *op. cit.,* 1914, pp. 48-49.

[34] Notes and Drafts, III-Df, Rodin Museum. And in the depersonalisation of the subject of the study and need for a time to listen. "As for myself, it is when sick that I loved a tree, a landscape" (Notes and Drafts, III-B-4, Rodin Museum).

[35] "Studying masterpieces requires solitude" (Rodin A., "Mon séjour à Rome", *Excelsior,* 18 February 1912, p. 2).

[36] Cladel J., *op. cit.,* 1903, p. 66.

24 - Bernès and Marouteau,
STUDIO IN THE ALMA PAVILION IN MEUDON,
(DETAIL)
gelatin silver print, Ph.9001.

linking the present to the past ...

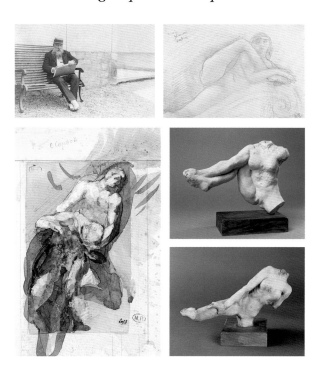

INDEPENDENT

"I felt as if I had always known him, that I was simply seeing him again: I found him smaller and yet more powerful, kinder, nobler. That forehead, the relationship between the forehead and nose coming out like a boat from its harbour … very strange. That forehead and nose have the style of stone. The mouth talks a language in a tone that is pleasant, close and juvenile. The laughter too, the laughter, both embarrassed and joyful, of a happy child." [1]

Anomymous,
PORTRAIT OF RODIN LAUGHING,
printing-out paper, 8 June 1902,
Ph.2033.

December 1862. A difficult but decisive month for Rodin. His sister Maria had just died of smallpox at the age of twenty-five, one year after entering a convent. Rodin was now alone. He spent several months in retreat with the Fathers of the Holy Sacrament to honour the memory of his sister, but sculpture, already a pressing need, imposed itself on him definitively. His solitude will always be associated with it, and the beginning of 1863, when he left the brotherhood, marked his independence.

It was almost six years after the last time he failed the entrance examination for the École des Beaux-Arts. Thanks to the major construction sites of Haussmann and the remodelling of Paris, there was a proliferation of workshops of ornamentalists and decorators. "When you are born a beggar, you have to carry a beggar's bag" [2], Rodin wrote simply to his aunt in 1860, as if this were an obvious but annoying fact. It was only later, when reviewing his past, that he acknowledged that those years of poverty had the merit of not giving him a choice. "The need to live forced me to learn every aspect of my craft. I have worked as a pointer, I have rough-hewn marble and stone, made ornaments and jewellery for a goldsmith for far too long, there is no doubt about that. […] But it was useful. I worked a lot for others. Those who were poor like me, with no assistance from the state, or stipend, worked everywhere and for everyone. It was a kind of apprenticeship in disguise. In succession, I made earrings for a jeweller and then decorative figures 3 metres high, and in this way I learned every branch of the craft." [3] The sculptor persisted because the hardships life imposed on him turned out to have beneficial effects. He was fully aware of this and brandished his former poverty like a lucky charm [4]. As a matter of fact, he always put forward his training as a craftsman to justify his

LEFT PAGE

Émile Sanremo,
RODIN ON A BENCH, DRAWING,
gelatin silver print, 1906, Ph.197.

Auguste Rodin,
PLUVIÔSE,
graphite and stump on buff paper,
between 1898 and 1910, D.1813.

Auguste Rodin,
STUDY FOR A SPANDREL (ÉCOINÇON),
graphite, pen, ink and gouache on
squared and pasted beige paper,
circa 1880 ? D.2053.

Auguste Rodin,
IRIS, MESSENGER OF THE GODS,
WITHOUT THE LEFT LEG,
terracotta, circa 1891, S.115.

Auguste Rodin,
FLYING FIGURE, SMALL SCALE MODEL,
terracotta, circa 1887, S.119.

1 Rilke R.M., letter to Clara Rilke, Paris, 11 rue Toullier, Tuesday, 2 September 1902, *Correspondance, Oeuvres 3*, Le Seuil, 1976, p. 24.

2 Rodin to Mrs. Hildiger, April, Meurthe et Moselle, [Paris, 11 August 1860], L. 745, Rodin Museum.

3 Dujardin-Beaumetz H., *op. cit.*, 1913, p. 81.

4 "And those who became great sculptors are those who were prevented by poverty or other difficult conditions and struggles from *succeeding* in schools. Because of these difficulties, they entered the workshop of Nature for a long but necessary apprenticeship." (Rodin A., *op. cit.*, 11 June 1910).

position on the fringe [5]. He now had permission to copy paintings at the Louvre, he continued his personal studies on morphology and sculpted in the family apartment.

Two meetings of capital importance marked the year 1864: Rose Beuret *(fig. 25)* and Albert-Ernest Carrier-Belleuse. Through her, he discovered that devotion had no limits, and through him he acquired financial security and learned how to be grateful. "Though I was making poor sculpture for Belleuse I was always thinking to myself about the composition of the figures and this helped me later on. I carried to the work I did for him the result of my study at home." [6]

The next decisive stage, in relation with his meeting with Rose, of course, was that Rodin left the family apartment to move into a stable nearby, in rue Lebrun, which he rented for one hundred and twenty francs a year. He was twenty-four years old at that point. Nearly fifty years later, he would remember his first studio in these terms. "The air filtered in from everywhere, through the badly closed windows, the wooden door that had become distorted; […] It was always icy cold; a well dug in one of the corners of the wall […] maintained a penetrating humidity in all seasons. Even now, I don't know how I was able to bear it! … That is where I made my *man with the broken nose.* […] The winter of that year was particularly harsh […]. The man with the broken nose froze and broke. The back of his head split and fell. I was only able to keep the mask, which I sent to the Salon; it was turned down." [7]

The model, Bibi, was a man from the neighbourhood who "had sunk to the position he then occupied through misfortune and drink" [8] *(fig. 26).* Looking back, Rodin confided: "That mask determined all my future work. It is the first good piece of modeling I ever did. From that time, I sought to look all around my work to draw it well in every aspect. I have kept that mask before my mind in everything I have done. I tried it on my first figure, 'The Bacchante,' but did not succeed; I tried it again on 'The Age of Brass', also without success, though it is a good figure. In fact, I have never succeeded in making a figure as good as 'The Broken Nose.'" [9]

[5] "I am", he said, "a worker who enjoys the vilest occupations. These rough hands here work the block, mix the plaster. I have retained the habits of a mason from my days as an apprentice. I am like the artists of the Renaissance: they were craftsmen and not refined gentlemen." (Rodin, quoted by Carillo G., "L'exemple de Rodin", *La Meuse-soir,* 1st February 1911). Rodin was always excessively preoccupied by matters relating to apprenticeship, as can be seen from the annotations in the margin of Chapter III, "L'Art décoratif" in the book *Art et démocratie* (Ollendorf 1912), dedicated to him by the author J. Paul-Boncour.

[6] Bartlett T.H., "Auguste Rodin sculptor", *The American Architect and Building News,* 26 January 1889, p. 44.

[7] Dujardin-Beaumetz H., *op. cit.,* 1913, pp. 115-116.

[8] Lawton F., *The Life and Works of Auguste Rodin,* London, T. Fisher Unwin, 1906, p. 25.

[9] Bartlett T.H., *op. cit,* 19 January 1889, p. 29.

The working conditions were hard in rue Lebrun. With no money to cast the clay figures, many sculptures were lost. Freedom was indeed a difficult apprenticeship! The *Bacchante*, his very first figure, which foreshadowed *The Age of Bronze* in its pose [10], was destroyed in a move. Rose posed for his first sculpted figure, but nothing remains of it for it was lost due to lack of money.

Rodin was now at the turning point of his work. From the portrait or figure modelled in the secrecy of his studio, to the parallel initiation into ornamentation and architecture, composition, variations of a same model, and commercial practices, Rodin was convinced of the idea that "a strong education of the eye and mind permits more imagination, more interpretation, greater skills in varying shapes and, particularly for those engaged in the decorative arts, it gives more freedom to vary profiles." [11]

In September 1870, he was enrolled in the National Guard, which had the task of resisting the encircling of the capital. This was no longer an appropriate period for decoration and after being discharged due to his myopia, he found himself destitute. When Carrier-Belleuse hired Rodin to follow him, he left "for Belgium, with great projects but not a penny." [12] Another move, and this time it led to a second crucial figure, *The Age of Bronze,* to which he owed his entire career by default. From that point onwards, Rodin intuitively chose the human body as the medium for his reflections on structure and light.

26 - Eugène Druet,
MAN WITH THE BROKEN NOSE,
albumen print, Ph.2299.

On his way to Italy at the end of 1875, he discovered the cathedral of Rheims, which he would see again later as "a huge figure of a women kneeling in prayer" [13]. This set in motion tireless exercises in observation that always brought him back to architecture as a universal law. "In the past, all I saw was the Gothic lace; I was fascinated by the magic of the ornamentation, which I thought was arbitrary. I did not know there was a scientific reason behind it, to soften and blur the lines. I can

---

[10] "It was in fact in the spirit of The *Age of Bronze*, Rodin told me, and Mme Rodin, who had posed for it standing up, she said, a hand on her head as if adjusting her hair, the other hanging down as if she had been using a mirror, could not think about it without very bitter memories, even after so many years." (Bénédite L., *op. cit.*, 1926, p. 16).

[11] Dujardin-Beaumetz H., *op. cit.*, 1913, p. 33.

[12] Tirel M., *Rodin intime*, Paris, published by Monde Nouveau, 1923, p. 9.

[13] Rodin A., *op. cit.*, 1914, p. 88.

27 - Anonymous,
THE LABOUR EXCHANGE IN BRUSSELS,
albumen print, Ph.12506.

28 - Auguste Rodin,
CARYATIDE ON THE BOULEVARD ANSPACH,
painted stucco, circa 1872 and 1874,
S.5707.

RIGHT PAGE
29 - Anonymous,
**MONUMENT TO CLAUDE LORRAIN IN THE
PÉPINIÈRE GARDEN IN NANCY,**
albumen print, touched up with ink
by Rodin, 1892, Ph.1851.

now understand its role and urgency; it swells the profiles, filling them with sap."[14] When the detail feeds the whole, when gradually, study by study, note by note, reflection by reflection, its only role is to contribute to the general fashioning of the structure, it makes it more legible, it conceals it in order to highlight it better[15].

His work with Carrier-Belleuse, and later with his partner Van Rasbourgh for the decoration of the Brussels Stock Exchange *(fig. 27)*, to which would soon be added other public buildings such as the Palace of the Academies or the caryatids along Boulevard Anspach *(fig. 28)*, again confronted Rodin with the question of integrating sculpted figures in a pre-existing architecture. The figure and the ornament merge, as when "at the ornamentalist M. Biais (he used to make) the figure that was inserted in the ornaments"[16]. He would continue this approach to incorporating a figure in a structure, as well considering the influence of the setting, when studying the pedestals for his sculptures much later. He applied these theories to the *Monument to Claude Lorrain* of 1892 *(fig. 29)* or the *Monument to Sarmiento*, commissioned in 1894: "[…] since about one century, we have taken it upon ourselves to close off works of art from the place for which they were created. There, in Museums, the spirit of centuries is mixed up with diverse manifestations. This

14 Cladel J., *op. cit.*, 7 November 1908, pp. 81-82.

15 "The ornament that is wrongly scorned is a synthesis, architecture

itself!", he would go as far as to confide to Coquiot (Coquiot G., *op. cit.*, 1917, p. 81).

16 Chéruy Collection, Library of Princeton University (United States).

31 - Auguste Rodin,
FLYING FIGURES OR BAUDELAIRE,
graphite, ink wash on paper pasted
on a printed medium, 1880-1888,
D.2002.

is what has made ornamentation lose its perfect meaning, in other words, the entire framework that should preoccupy an artist when he makes a work for a given setting. We have thus ended up, rather rapidly, by considering artworks as objects that can be placed just about anywhere. This is unfortunate because art should not be an embellishment but a well established ornamentation which must be part of a harmonious whole." [17] However, he would need a lifetime to master the relationship between the figure and its environment, until finally, apart from the *Balzac* and its relationship with space that seemed to have been resolved, *The Gates of Hell* were erected [18].

In 1880, the commission for the *Gates* gave Rodin an opportunity to surpass the work of his youth and training and transform it into a permanent work, which would develop at the same time as his research and, like it, remain unfinished. The unresolved problem of the border *(fig. 30)*, of the transition represented by the frame, is a recurring one in the drawings of the same period. He liked to paste them in the printed frames of the catalogue of a fabric firm, thus giving a foundation for

30 - Auguste Rodin,
LEFT SIDE OF THE PEDIMENT OF THE GATES OF HELL,
plaster, circa 1890, S.5777.

17 Canudo R., "La crise des "Métiers": Les Idées d'Auguste Rodin", *L'Opinion*, 4 February 1911.

18 For details, see Le Normand-Romain A., *Rodin, The Gates of Hell*, Paris, Rodin Museum Publications, 2002.

32 - Auguste Rodin,
**COLUMN-STATUES ON THE LEFT SPLAY OF
THE SOUTHERN PORTAL OF THE SAINT
JULIEN CATHEDRAL IN LE MANS**
graphite, pen and black ink on a notebook
page, between 1901 and 1909?
D.6337, notebook 5, f°7 r°.

the sinuous silhouettes *(fig. 31)*. All his previous drawings, which he drowned in ink as he delved further into Dante's *Inferno*, were the first pretexts for concentrating on structure. The backing for these "black" drawings were sheets of paper taken from accounting ledgers, with ruled orthogonal lines that enclosed and intensified the cut-out or printed friezes, already lending themselves to in-depth reflection on the frame. These drawings, most of which he said were related to the *Inferno*, can probably be perceived as the premises of this reflection on the structure of the *Gate* and the incorporation of figures *(fig. 32, 34 and 35)*.

In this instance, the figure and the architecture blend into one and the same work, a precise synthesis of research carried out over a lifetime. Where one or the other was used to complete each other, they now merged. "I always searched for the architectural aspect of a body. And really, I did not look for it, it is there, it appears every instant, one has but to look. The human body, freed of its movements […] is a vivid lesson that nature, in its endless generosity, offers to our architecture. The secret is in movement, in the planes. All art is based on planes. A plane is the close relationship between all things in a whole" [19] *(fig. 33)*. And he finally managed to write on a loose sheet of paper that "sculpture is architecture too, and one should only speak of it by this name" [20].

As a pretext for research on the human body, Rodin viewed movement as the accomplishment of studies on the figure, and beyond it, all structures. From *The Falling Man* to *The Walking Man* or *The Flying Figure*, the descriptive titles indicate there is nothing more to say [21]. Life evolves through movement, hence the freedom expressed by the models moving around in the studio. Rodin was continually on the lookout, and with his pencil he tracked the intervening period with the single-minded purpose of capturing truthful observation. "I like to draw because it is a procedure that seizes movements faster than sculpture. It fixes fleeting truth almost instantaneously. It can sometimes happen that I set aside my roughing chisel for two whole weeks and only handle a pencil and paintbrush. I draw without interruption … I draw by day … by a lamp … When I feel [fatigue] approaching, I stop drawing and go back to sculpture. The change of occupation relaxes me […] And my joy is even greater to feel free inside me, that is to say, emancipated from all artistic lies." [22]

[19] Canudo R., *op. cit.*, 5 April 1913, p. 27.

[20] Notes and Drafts, I, Rodin Museum.

[21] Frequently suggested by friends who were writers or critics, Rodin's titles were usually added later because the work itself had no need for a subject. In this, he differed from most of his contemporaries who considered literary or mythological references to be important.

[22] Gsell P., "Rodin raconté par lui-même", *La Revue*, 1st May 1906, pp. 99-100.

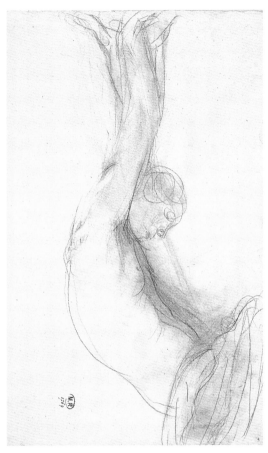

33 - Auguste Rodin,
TORSO OF A NUDE WOMAN, LEFT PROFILE,
ARMS STRETCHED ABOVE HER HEAD,
graphite and stump on buff watermarked
paper, D.1764.

34 - **CAST OF SPANDREL,**
plaster, Co.1832.

35 - Auguste Rodin,
SPANDREL: EROS AND PSYCHE,
graphite and watercolour on buff paper,
D.4109.

a life filled to the brim …

SENSUAL

"And near a window, one single customer: a robust old man with a flowing beard and wrinkled forehead, who had tied his napkin around his neck like a baby. Whenever his napkin shifted, one could catch a glimpse of a small red patch on the silk lapel of his frock coat. […] a rectangular forehead beneath short cut hair full wide eyes under lowered eyelids, like those of a Virgin by Da Vinci, a pink complexion, a nose narrow at the bridge and flared out at the tip and, above all, an undulating beard with amber reflections"[1].

He needed solitude. For his work, of course, but also outside the time he spent on his sculpture. It was like a *sine qua non* condition for being available to things, for a more acute awareness, for greater receptivity in a happiness that is reflected in some of his later notes[2]. Paradoxically, it was only under such circumstances that Rodin, in his introspection, could open himself to the external world, to draw nourishment from it, and by slowly digesting the visible, grow richer.

" … leaning on the window sill, I bathe my forehead in the morning mist, and the thoughts of my affairs disappear, a blackbird sings and already his song is over, but the loving atmosphere of spring resounds with the chirping of hundreds of birds. […] such gentle creation penetrates me and my soul returns to its place in nature, and when I go downstairs, the dogs will flatter me – and in the meantime, my population of statues are waiting for me, to display themselves and work with me"[3].

He nevertheless needed the serenity that comes with age to accept that those times were not lost. "I admire peacefully, which is impossible when one is young. The period of youth is more feverish, it has an agitation that does not leave you time to see"[4], he confided in 1903. In the memories of his younger days, time was constantly shortened by his daily work, leaving no room for any other occupation[5]. In fulfilling the promise he made to himself to accomplish his art by first mastering a technique, nothing else existed apart from this unflagging work. And rest, which gave him a guilty feeling because he still associated it with wastefulness, was

R. Moreau,
PORTRAIT OF RODIN SEATED,
printing-out paper with mat collodion,
1907 ? Ph.705.

LEFT PAGE

Auguste Rodin,
TORSO OF ADÈLE,
terracotta, circa 1882-1883, S.1177.

Auguste Rodin,
STUDY FOR THE KISS,
Terracotta, circa 1881-1882, S.3895.

Auguste Rodin,
THE ETERNAL IDOL,
plaster, cast of the marble, 1893, S.1044.

Cl. Gerschel,
RODIN CARESSING THE MARBLE STATUE OF HERCULES,
gelatin silver print, 1913 ? Ph.873.

Auguste Rodin,
SEATED WOMAN, HALF-CLOTHED,
graphite and watercolour on buff paper,
D.5010.

---

1 Georges-Michel M., "Le sculpteur et l'avion. Comment Rodin symbolise l'envol du biplan …", *Comoedia*, 6 May 1913.

2 "What a mild Sunday! I am not working but I have time for myself, inhaling this caress that I do not want to leave." (Notes and Drafts, Xb 15, Rodin Museum).

3 Notes and Drafts, IIIDa-2, Rodin Museum.

4 Cladel J., *op. cit.*, 1903, p. 56.

5 "I went through my daily fourteen hours of work and I only rested on Sundays. On that day, my wife and I would go to some open-air café for a big meal costing three francs for both of us, and this was our only reward for the week!" (Coquiot G., *op. cit.*, 1917, pp. 25-26).

confused with boredom. "As a child, when I was sick, I would hear the morning tradesmen. I had the feeling that I should have been at work" [6]. At the age of seventy-three, he again said, as if repeating a secret: "I would find it unbearable not to produce. Rest is monotonous, and has the dreariness of all that comes to an end" [7]. It required a very subtle evolution to understand that his relationship with the visible, intensified during moments of rest, was also part of his work. It took sixty years to complete, on reaching an age when he was able to master everything, when life had taken it upon itself to prove that he no longer needed to justify himself.

36 - Anonymous,
RODIN IN THE DINING ROOM IN MEUDON,
printing-out paper, Ph.788.

His notebooks were always in his pocket, if only to note down the bliss of being an integral part of the nature he venerated so much, but with an attitude that was quite different from the one that led him to work on the actual form of the visible. He described "this vast rotunda where I eat simply as if in a dairy. This velvety moss on this green softened by tiny star shoots, like in the sky, the mottled ground streaking between my feet, that advance beneath me, when I walk like the rotation of the earth, I blame the melancholy of the hour" [8]. Apart from observing, he lived life to the full. To the point of daring to write to others in *Montjoie!* on 10 February 1913: "Living in the moral time of branches, merging with one's fellow creatures, falling into line, the heart in unison, implies contributing to something great under a shared sky" [9].

And so he immersed himself in nature, for it alone could distract him from his sculpture and allow him to go back to it revived, and vice versa. He brought flowers into the house, surrounding the window frames or as bouquets on the table. There were many accounts about the sculptor's incredible ability to turn his free moments,

[6] Notes and Drafts, VIDc-11, Rodin Museum.

[7] Dujardin-Beaumetz H., *op. cit.*, 1913, p. 93.

[8] Notebook n° 59, f° 67 v° and 68 r°, Rodin Museum.

[9] Rodin A., "Promenades dans la forêt de Meudon", *Montjoie!*, 10 February 1913.

suspended between two activities, into a time of pure enjoyment and intense receptivity. Paul Gsell, who published his conversations with Rodin in 1911, and Mario Meunier, his secretary, both describe how he behaved, turning the reality that surrounded him into his own, and appropriating the beautiful at the same time as the good. "He had positioned his bed in such a way that even when lying down, he could see the sinuous course of the Seine lazily flowing towards the Pont de Sèvres and the bell tower of Saint-Cloud in the distance." [10] During his meals, he placed antique objects and flowers before him to accompany his earthly meals, which he tasted with pleasure *(fig. 36)*. Rodin was a sensualist. "Rodin liked to arrange small torsos and little antique busts in the midst of the flowers and greenery that decorated the table at which he ate. On other occasions, a Greek vase, taken from his museum, was set in front of him, or else a Tanagra Victory, or a dancer from Myrrha. The meals were always very simple but delicious: "Alas, Rodin frequently told me, we have lost all our excellent traditions, even the one – the last we should have lost – of good French cooking! I no longer know where to eat in Paris. No matter where I go, I cannot find anywhere the natural taste of ingredients for they have been too highly seasoned during cooking, or peppered with chemicals. […] For a person like me who has always loved good wine, I think it is criminal to deliberately grow poorer by depriving ourselves of a sense. Even in good health, we only have just enough to appreciate and feel the immensity of life. One must be sick to cut down, and to mutilate oneself is always a crime. Whatever medicine dictates, I always drink wine, especially red wine, from Roussillon and from Burgundy. I drink in moderation but I drink good wine, and I feel very well after drinking it, so well that I end up believing that Bacchus takes his revenge on drinkers of water by depriving them of enthusiasm, and to be an artist one must love wine!" [11] *(fig. 37)*.

37 - Anonymous,
RODIN AT TABLE IN JEAN DOLENT'S HOME,
printing-out paper, 30 July 1899,
Ph.146.

[10] Gsell P., "Le musée Rodin à Meudon", *La Renaissance de l'art français et des Industries de luxe,* Paris, August 1923, p. 458.

[11] Meunier M., "Rodin intime", *La Semaine littéraire,* 21 September 1918.

38 - Eugène Druet,
RODIN HOLDING AN EGYPTIAN STATUETTE,
gelatin silver print, 1914 ? Ph.833.

To go back to Meudon, he preferred travelling by boat than by train, and took "his carriage" [12] at the Pont de l'Alma because it allowed him to daydream while admiring the sunsets. On summer evenings he used to read books of past centuries all by himself in the garden of the Hôtel Biron: "He stroked the precious bindings, he savoured the exquisite typography and the weighty maxims. And to make sure he was not disturbed, he would let loose his German dog, Dora, who constantly snarled, with her black lips curled over her long white teeth." [13] Nothing was more natural for a sculptor than this physical relationship with the world, developed from a very early age, by drawing before even working on volume through matter.

There is no doubt that being short sighted led him into new territories. It may even have helped him develop an extraordinary sense of touch in compensation [14] (*fig. 38).* After the sense of sight, it is by caresses that he appropriated forms, and it is his hand that conveyed emotions and understanding, as in the case of the "sparrow-hawk, an Egyptian masterpiece, [...] that Rodin held between his hands, and which had such a marvellous shape, such a harmonious understanding, that it still seemed to be quivering under the caress of his fingers. [...] This is what brought to my attention Rodin's intense vision, because he completely possessed it with that caress. I believe that on the days when fatigue would overcome his muscles, the sculptor recovered his strength and direction by touching the fluttering wings of the eternal bird" [15], relates the author of the first book published about Rodin in 1899. Likewise, the sculptor Jules Desbois caught him unawares placing a kiss on the belly of a model at the end of a session [16].

From touching to seeing, from seeing and then touching, the two senses combined were the conditions for creation, linking art and manner in a constantly unappeased pleasure, in a feverish excitement channelled into diligent work. Such an acute appreciation of the gentleness of a volume and the truth of an outline can only be achieved by adopting a universal approach that depersonalises the subject and transforms it into an object of all that is possible. Gsell confirms this, quoting Rodin, who had invited him, for the pleasure of the eyes and appreciation of the contour, to observe his antiques in the light of a lamp: "if I move the lamp in all directions, I make fugitive shadows pulsate over the marble, which finally end up by resting permanently once the lamp stops moving... Oh, what joy!" [17] "You should

[12] Cladel J., *op. cit.,* 1903, p. 30.

[13] Gsell P., "Les jardins de l'Hôtel Biron", *Bref,* 22 December 1927.

[14] Numerous personal notes reveal the simplification of values and planes in the distance. For example, "My myopia makes me see this Christ with admirable Byzantine details. Everything is modelled." (Notes and Drafts, XBa-9, Rodin Museum). "When you are short-sighted you think everything bathes in milky water" (Notebook n° 96, f°15 v°, Rodin Museum). "When I wear my glasses, it is as precise as an engraving by Vernet, and when I take them off, it is a mass of fortunate effects with the appearance of a marine monster leaving its tail plunged in the sea" (Notebook n° 75, f°39 v°, Rodin Museum).

[15] Maillard L., *op. cit.,* 1899, p. 39.

[16] Cladel J., *op. cit.,* 1936, p. 271.

[17] Notes and Drafts ; 1912, XBa-22, Rodin Museum.

[18] Gsell P., *op. cit.,* 1st May 1906, p. 93.

come back here one night: we will move a lamp over these forms and you will then discover all the imperceptible undulations of the contours quivering on this flesh, which is so simple in appearance. It is fantastic! This is life! When you feel it, you say to yourself, 'How strange, why isn't it warm?'"[18] And after the eye, the hand marked the final possession. While the eyes kissed, the hand embraced. When combined with Rodin's excessively sensual temperament, this voluptuous matter, with its vibrant modelling, plunged him into an instantaneously physical world. And creation was the immediate and primary outcome. Even though he dressed his models in 18th century clothes of faded colours, bought from a second-hand dealer, "when the cloaks open, they reveal opaline flesh and seem to be like sepals *(sic)* half-opening on to budding flowers. I firmly believe that for Rodin this diabolical touch, which added spice to the spectacle, is what heightened the flavour", added Paul Gsell[19]. Anonymous models, objects of fantasies, worldly women who came to pose for a bust, students or patrons, there were many who spoke of a relationship with the sculptor. A figment of the imagination? Isadora Duncan and Anna de Noailles had no hesitation in describing the unambiguous attitude of Rodin during their visits or posing sessions[20].

In the end, it did not matter what really happened in the intimacy of his studio. When all is said and done, Rodin was a seducer. Wreathed in glory, he used and abused it, and he had the perfect excuse: his work. And with paper for the skin and clay for the flesh, the borderline was maintained. The sculptor-courtier, who was courted, amassed his conquests. "I started on the road with only one companion, and at the end of my career, I had a group, a group that served me. I am no longer vigorous but they escort me[21]. And if the amorous rituals on Thursday afternoons at the Palais d'Orsay, described by his secretaries after 1904, were a secret shared among rare followers, his reputation was already forged. In 1897, when his assistant Pézieux, used the pithy turn of phrase, "Il est tellement queutif, le bougre!"[22], he was only saying out loud what all of Paris had been whispering for more than ten

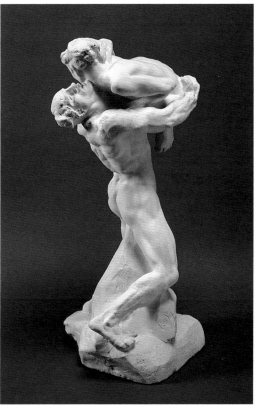

39 - Auguste Rodin,
I AM BEAUTIFUL,
plaster, 1885 ? S.1292.

19 Gsell P., *Douze aquarelles d'Auguste Rodin*, Paris, George & Cie., 1920, p. 19.

20 "He showed his works with the simplicity of the very great. Sometimes he murmured the name for his statues, but one felt that names meant little to him. He ran his hands over them, and caressed them. I remember thinking that beneath his hands the marble seemed to flow like molten lead. Finally he took a small quantity of clay and pressed it between his palms. he breathed hard as he did

so. The heat streamed from him like a radiant furnace. In a few moments he had formed a woman's breast that palpitated beneath his fingers.[…] he gazed at me with lowered lids, his eyes blazing, and then, with the same expression that he had before his works, he came toward me. He ran his hands over my nake, breast, stroken my arms and ran his hands over my hips, my bare legs and feet. He began to knead my whole body as if it were clay, while from him emanated heat that scorched and melted me. My whole desire was to yield to him my

entire being and, indeed, I would have done so if it had not been that my absurd up-bringing caused me to become frightened and I withdrew, threw my dress over my tunic and sent him away bewildered" (Duncan I., *My life*, New York, garden City Publishing compagny, 1927, p.90).

21 Notes and Drafts, XBa-27, Rodin Museum.

22 Comment by Jean Alexandre Pézieux about Rodin in 1897, in Jeanès J.E.S., *op. cit.*, 1946, p. 138.

years. In 1886, the Georges Petit gallery, which liked to exhibit the works of bold artists, had no hesitation in displaying three "Studies on Human Tutting", which included *I am Beautiful (fig. 39)*.

The figures from Dante in *The Gates of Hell* assumed a sensuality that was typical of Baudelaire in *Les Fleurs du Mal*. "[Rodin] seemed to be intoxicated by it. In a burst of spontaneous speed, he created numerous damned women who emerged, palpitating, from his fingers. Some of them lived for one hour and then were put back into the thick reworked clay. Others, we did not want to die and we friends named them, in passing, Phryne, Hera, Sappho and Phedra, all victims of legends of love and all damned souls who fled eternally from 'that infinity they bore within themselves'"[23] *(figs. 40 and 41)*. Parisians were thus exposed to his sensuality. The "disquieting originality" of those "couplings that no other sculptor had dared to treat before" aroused criticism on the occasion of a joint exhibition with Monet in 1889"[24]. However, in an era when literature, widely recognised as being erotic, flourished through the pens of such writers such as Pierre Louys or Barbey d'Aurevilly, or when the obscene stereo-photographs by Belloc were discovered and strongly criticised, the more sex became fashionable the more it was censured. The public, in viewing Rodin's works, did not avert its eyes. The couples of *The Gates of Hell* provided an ideal outlet. The scandal was not focused on the theme

41 - Eugène Druet,
FUGIT AMOR,
gelatin silver print, Ph.1988.

LEFT PAGE

40 - Auguste Rodin,
ASSEMBLAGE: VARIATION OF THE CROUCHING WOMAN AND THE MARTYR,
plaster, circa 1889-1890, S.64.

23 Le Roux H., "La vie à Paris", *Le Temps*, 20 June 1889.   **24** Maus O., *L'Art Moderne*, 1889.

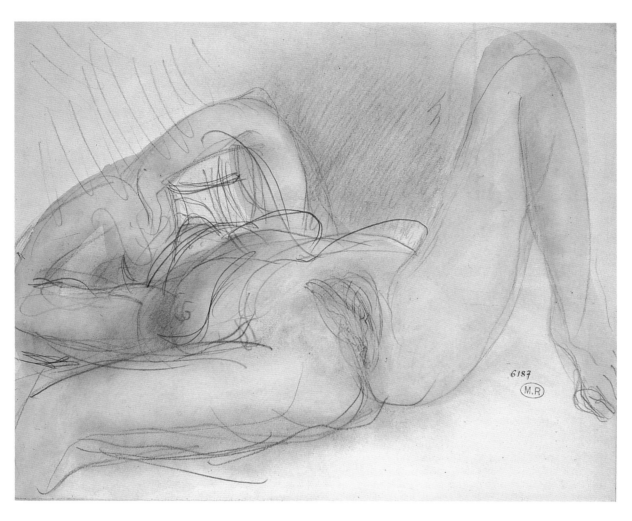

42 - Auguste Rodin,
**NUDE WOMAN VIEWED FROM THE FRONT,
ARMS AND LEGS FOLDED AND SPREAD OUT,**
graphite and watercolour on buff paper,
D.6187.

but on the form. The sculptor was unmoved by the occasional attacks on the obscenity of his works: "[…] the desire to create a voluptuous work is legitimate. […] Evoking the thrills of desire aroused by living flesh through purely artistic means is quite the opposite of pornography"[25]. Yet being concerned about his image, he said very little on the subject. "You are well aware that my enemies frequently call me a satyr and a sodomite. I am hardly surprised. These are the kind of accusations the envious easily throw at masters whose talent they can hardly deny. However, I do not want to be seen supplying them with arms to use against me."[26] This is why he only allowed a few friends to see his boldest statuettes and drawings *(fig. 42)*. In his den in Meudon, "he would ask them to follow him up some wooden stairs in the corner of the vast hall. They led to a gallery with a cupboard. He would open this cupboard ceremoniously and take out some small terracotta figures. They

[25] Rodin, quoted by Varin M., "Un Conseil de l'Ordre pour les Artistes", *Comoedia*, 9 January 1911.

[26] Gsell P., *op. cit.*, 1920, pp. 14-15.

[27] *Idem*, p. 14.

[28] "I did not know that although I scorned them (women) when I was twenty years old, they would charm me at the age of seventy. I scorned them because I was shy …" (Cladel J., *op. cit.*, 1936, p. 301).

[29] Cladel J., *op. cit.*, 1903, p. 56.

[30] Gsell P., *op. cit.*, 1920, p. 9.

[31] Gsell P., *op. cit.*, 1920, p. 11

were delightfully immodest. He showed them to his guests. Or else he handed them over, taking the trouble to turn them in their hands to make them admire every aspect."[27] *(fig. 43)*.

However, Rodin did not fail to live up to his reputation. He even played on it but by claiming the need for beauty and the search for expressions of life. Innocence personified, if one were to believe him. Fulfilled in his art, he was now free to do anything without giving the impression of being involved. This was the exact opposite of his youth as a shy ascetic[28], growing up under the rigorous influence of his mother and castrating effects of his sister. As for Rose, she had absolutely no say in the matter. She crystallised the "admirable" woman, capable of complete devotion and invincible energy"[29], whose path crossed those who, on their own, accompanied him during his early years. It was as if feelings and pleasure were incompatible. He was never capable of reconciling the two in his lifetime, except perhaps during his flaming passion for Camille Claudel, backed by constant work. It was so incredibly powerful that it nourished their strong emotions and sculpture for fifteen years. He was still unable to channel the energy that had prevented him, when he was young, from having another relationship, and this is precisely

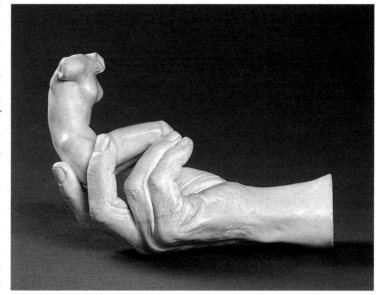

43 - Paul Cruet,
CAST OF RODIN'S HAND HOLDING A FEMALE TORSO,
plaster, 1917, S.839.

NEXT DOUBLE PAGE

Louis Morin,
RODIN SCULPTING IN HIS STUDIO,
black ink and watercolour on buff paper, 1900, D.7695.

what made such success possible. Although in those days work was his refuge, even an escape, when he was older he used it as a pretext to conquer women in great numbers, honourably, and as a keen collector. What is more, he did not even have to try hard. It was not completely his fault. If art opened the doors to the Salons for him, it also opened the doors to bedrooms.

During his youth, the act of creation was a necessary palliative for a stifled libido. When he finally expressed it, it was because his work had become free and he had acquired the assurance of a man with savoir-faire. He would enjoy both art and pleasure with the same insatiable appetite. In fact, as he would later confide to Paul Gsell: "In the final analysis, art is but voluptuous pleasure. It is only a derivative of the power of loving."[30] "Art, I tell you, is just a form of love. […] Oh, I know only too well that prudish moralists will put their hands over their ears. But I will nevertheless say out loud what all artists think. […] Desire! Desire! What a wonderful stimulant!"[31]

The ultimate justification, but he needed a long time to get there.

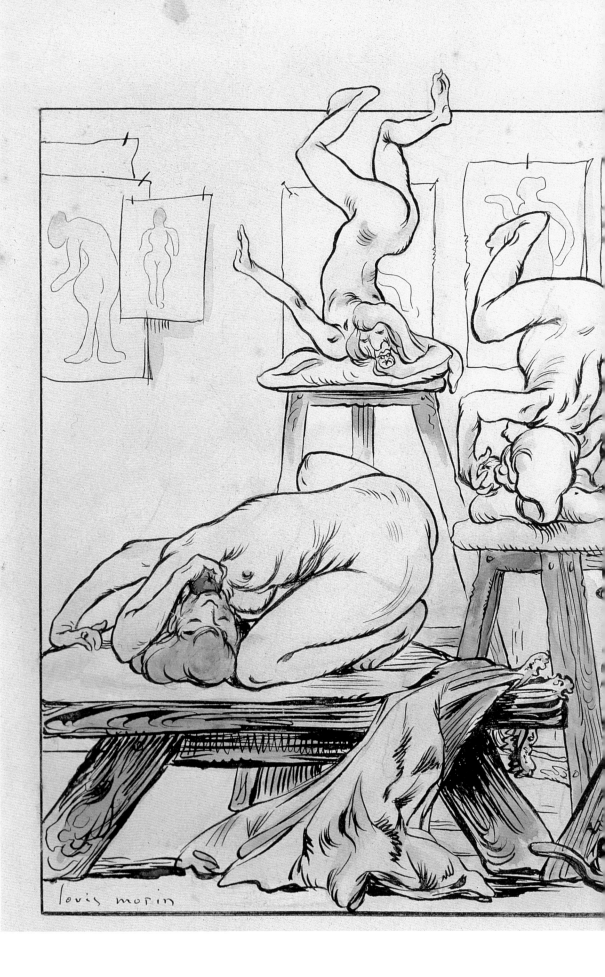

seeing … seeing …, and understanding

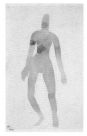

CURIOUS

"A man of medium height, Rodin's massive torso bore a head with a strangely receding and rocky forehead, a bony nose with powerful nostrils, silky white hair, the beard of a marine god, and small eyes narrowed by myopia, sometimes piercing and sharp, like the expression of a faun, and sometimes gentle and clear like a wild flower." [1]

Walter Henry Barnett,
RODIN (DETAIL),
carbon print, 1904,
Ph.1095.

Rodin's fame arrived at the same time as the 20th century and its accelerated advances. Major revolutions in progress and comfort, from the car to the plane, from electricity to telephones, from phonographs to the cinema, from vaccinations to X-rays, achieved the unachievable. In his speech as president of a banquet in honour of Paul Adam [2], on the evening of 11 December 1906, he spoke with concern of the "audacity of the times and sciences […] during a period resembling a cataclysm", "this furnace of present times and […] its dazzling speed in which the gods and men of the future are re-formed in a melting pot." [3] Totally engrossed in his work at the beginning of the century, he distanced himself as much as possible from the effects of industrialisation, which had started to invade him, by paying more and more tributes to nature. Torn between obvious improvements in comfort and its consequences, he noted for himself on an undated slip of paper, "The century is a child prodigy […] days of poetry, what have become of you" [4]. His position was clear on the eve of the First World War: "What a sorry time we live in! Some believe in progress because there are telephones, steamer, etc. But all that is only an improvement of the arm, the leg, the eye, the ear. Who shall improve the soul, which will soon disappear?" [5] "Tranquillity is a landscape in itself. Who believed that the world was material? […] The car arrives with the noise of a cascade… This new monster, the car" [6]. Rodin never owned one, or a telephone either, and he continued to harness his old horse Ran-tan-plan to go to the Meudon railway station and catch the train for Paris and his studios.

LEFT PAGE

Auguste Rodin,
TORSO OF AN ADOLESCENT IN DESPAIR,
terracotta, circa 1882, S.1803.

Léopold Reutlinger,
**PORTRAIT OF RODIN WITH A PINCE-NEZ,
A HAND ON HIS BEARD,**
albumen print, 1897, Ph.85.

Auguste Rodin,
**NUDE WOMAN STANDING,
VIEWED FROM THE FRONT,**
graphite and watercolour on buff paper
pasted on cardboard, D.4672.

Etruscan art,
EPHEBE,
bronze, 3rd-2nd century B.C., Co.1329.

SHELLS,
Co. 3054, 3055, 3056.

Egyptian art,
TORSO OF NECTANEBO I,
quartzite, 30th dynasty (380-342 B.C.),
Co.1420.

[1] Meunier M., *op. cit.*, 21 September 1918.

[2] A man of letters and a journalist (1862-1920).

[3] Notes and Drafts, IIIDe, Rodin Museum.

[4] Notes and Drafts, IIIB-4, Rodin Museum.

[5] Williamson Kennedy, *W.E. Henley, A Memoir*, London, Harold Shaylor, 1930, pp. 251-252. "Our industrial century only moved faster than the horse by imitating, if somewhat superficially, the shape of animals that run: a train is indeed in the image of an animal with four feet, and a car too. Aviation made no advances, as long as it remained in the grotesque shape of a ball, which has no meaning in nature. Now, it imitates the shape of birds, and it advances in an astonishing way, and the same applies to submarines. One must imitate nature, one must copy it. But it is necessary to know that *copying* means *understanding and interpreting.*" (Rodin, quoted by Canudo R., *op. cit*, 5 April 1913, p. 38).

[6] Rodin A., *op. cit.*, 10 February 1913.

44 - Anonymous,
RODIN LOOKING AT THE SKY,
ROSE BEURET (DETAIL),
gelatin silver negative on glass,
Ph.7753.

Only aviation fascinated him[7] *(fig. 44)*. The "dream of Da Vinci", as he liked to call it, deserved every effort and sacrifice, especially as it appeared in time to defend France. In fact, in 1912, he donated a copy of his *Defence* to aviation, for the acquisition of a military plane. In Rodin's view, aviation was an extension, an outcome: "The cross of cathedrals pierced the sky. Young men climb it. Everything gives way to it, so how can one talk of other achievements?"[8] This is what was of interest to him *(fig. 45)*.

[7] "It looks as if human ingenuity has concentrated on industry. This has led to astonishing aviation. But nearly everything has been forgotten about art. People want to ignore it." (Rodin, quoted by Canudo R., *op. cit.,* 5 April 1913, p. 27).

[8] "Mil neuf cent dix - ce que l'Année dernière lègue à l'Année qui vient.", *Paris-Journal,* 1st January 1911, p. 2. Rodin pointed out: "I had a plan.

He protected himself against the accelerated speed of his period by taking refuge in the immutability of his art, in the eternity of the Ancients, in the universality of nature. He was only in tune with his century when he found in it an echo of his research. This is what he called "understanding". Rodin was curious because he was always seeking proof about the foundation of things and their place during those times of folly. He looked for reassurance, the guarantee of the eternity of art, the durability of its principles. Anything new was therefore a motif for reflection and was likely to stimulate his questioning on the accuracy of a line. It was a matter of seeing, by undertaking a vertical and refined search instead of a horizontal and perpetual quest.

Rodin was accustomed to doing this. He had been searching since his childhood, even before he was capable of putting a word to things. He described, with the objective outlook of his old age, his chance encounter with

45 · Eugène Druet,
THE "BIPLANE" BY RODIN :
THE BENEDICTIONS, IN THE COURTYARD
OF THE MARBLE DEPOSITORY,
gelatin silver print, 1894,
Ph.2752.

Michelangelo one day, in his neighbourhood library near the Pantheon, around 1853: It was like a revelation for me. The following day, I asked for the book again, and was immediately consumed by a desire to model works like those I had seen. I had found my vocation" [9]. The years of study after 1854 also gave him his first food for thought, which nothing could stop. His curiosity initially focused on those works that had survived through the ages to reach him. In 1875, it pushed him to move out of his immediate environment and travel to Italy for his first trip, like Carpeaux twenty years earlier. In Naples, he found "an Apollo with a leg in exactly the same pose as the one of my *Age of Bronze*, which had taken me six months of work. I studied it and saw that although on the surface everything seemed to be succinct, in reality all the muscles were constructed and all the details could be seen coming to life one by one. This is because the ancients studied everything from the profile, from all the profiles in succession" [10]. Two years later, after returning from Belgium, he set off for the first time to explore the cathedrals of France. Without even being aware of it, he was searching for the meeting point between sculpture and architecture, and in turn between architecture and its environment, which he would put to the test in his *Gates of Hell*. Right from the start of his artistic career,

The *Benedictions* from heaven. To erect it on the tomb of the modern Icarus!" In fact, he called this work "my biplane". (Georges-Michel M., *op. cit.*, 6 May 1913).

[9] Cheruy R., *op. cit.*, 20 January 1929.

[10] Rodin A., "La leçon de l'Antique", *Le Musée*, January–February 1904, p. 16. He was

probably referring to the *Doryphorus* by Polyclitus, belonging to the National Museum of Naples.

47 - Auguste Rodin,
**NUDE MAN VIEWED FROM THE BACK,
LEANING AGAINST A PEDESTAL
AND RAISING A CROWN,**
pen, ink and ink wash on pasted buff paper,
circa 1880 ? D.449.

46 - Indian art,
**SCULPTED PANEL : BEARDLESS ARCHER
TAKING AIM,**
teak wood, 17th and 18th centuries,
Co.110.

Rodin had an intuition when viewing sculpture, from the antiquities at the Louvre to Michelangelo, and then the cathedrals. He found it by searching carefully and was thus able to lay the foundation of his work. And he spent the rest of his life testing it.

When Japonism swept over artistic circles in France and the taste for the exotic had reached its peak, the objects he collected from 1890 onwards were selected mainly for their formal characteristics. In this case too, Rodin put his finger on something. From wooden components of Indian carts to Japanese masks, from stencils to perfume burners, from engravings to netsukes [11], he was attracted by a variety of objects. And by looking more closely, it is easy to understand why *(figs. 46 to 49)*. Although they were not the only objects of his curiosity, they were a perfect

demonstration of his inquiring mind. First of all, there were the Javanese dances at the Universal Exhibition in 1889, which he remembered more clearly than the great attraction of that event: the marvellous fountains coloured with electric lighting that were displayed on the Champ de Mars under the recently built Eiffel tower. In 1900, during the big Universal Exhibition of Paris, on the fringe of which he had set up his first personal exhibition in France, journalists from *La Presse* asked Rodin what he considered to be the "highlight of the exhibition". Rodin, who was already famous by then, had no hesitation in replying "I think my most vivid impression was of the Far East section. The Cambodian staircase and the bas-reliefs from the Sino-Dutch Monastery seemed to me to be a marvellous art, unknown until now, and then the exotic dances, especially Loïe Fuller and, with her, Sada Yacco, with such a vibrant art, such incredible perfection".[12] He forgot to mention the Indochinese pagoda even though he had signed a petition to preserve it.

48 - Japanese art,
JAPANESE MASK,
stained wood covered in a reddish coating, 19th century, Co.130.

49 - Auguste Rodin,
CRYING WOMAN,
ceramic, 1889, S.611.

[11] A netsuke is an indispensable accessory of the traditional Japanese costume that serves as a counter-weight to objects attached to the belt.

[12] "Le Clou de l'exposition", *La Presse*, 13 October 1900.

50 - Emile Sanremo,
RODIN SKETCHING THE CAMBODIAN DANCERS,
gelatin silver print, July 1906,
Ph.14379.

51 - Auguste Rodin,
**CAMBODIAN DANCER, HALF-BODY WITH
STRETCHED ARMS,**
graphite and gouache on buff paper,
July 1906, D.4430.

52 - Auguste Rodin,
CAMBODIAN DANCER, RIGHT PROFILE,
graphite, watercolour, gouache
and soft lead pencil on buff paper,
July 1906, D.4480.

In 1906, the sinuous dancing of the royal ballet of Cambodia, on tour in France, filled him with wonder *(fig. 50)*. Because exoticism is an interaction between space and time, in principle contradictory, and because it conveyed strangeness and curiosity, Rodin turned it into yet another launching pad for his research[13]. Immediately recycled into his work, the movements of Cambodian dance, "of a strange and marvellous appeal"[14], became the subject not only of numerous drawings but also of notes and interviews. A series of watercolour sheets of these small dancers have survived but they no longer reflect the intense emotion that gripped the sculptor on seeing such grace, which was a complete novelty in his eyes *(fig. 51)*. It is particularly touching that he should have received a lesson on movement in such a natural way by children, and it explains the gifts, toys and shoes he gave them somewhat awkwardly, almost like some kind of compensation. "They brought the antique to life for me. […] they gave me fresh reasons to believe that nature is an inexhaustible source for those who drink from it […]. I am a man who has devoted all his life to studying nature, and who has constantly admired works from antiquity. Just imagine my reaction to such a complete show that gave me back antiquity by unveiling mysteries! […] In my opinion, I am sure that my vision broadened when I watched them; I saw higher and further; finally, I learned …"[15].

This is where Rodin's curiosity lay: he needed to understand in order to learn, and to absorb what he had learned. Discovering the Far East echoed his experience with Greece, which he knew so well by then, for it matched and complemented it. During that same year, in 1906, the big angel on the sundial of the Chartres cathedral inevitably "found its match in Cambodia" in the eyes of the sculptor *(figs. 52 and 53)*. "The same thought has safeguarded art in Athens, in Chartres and in Cambodia, everywhere"[16]. The great principle, the one governing "the unity of nature"[17] through time and space was established. And exoticism had died.

Even if Hanako still remained. In 1906, the Japanese dancer performed *Death of a Geisha* at the Colonial Exhibition in Marseilles, where Rodin had followed the little dancers. Her extraordinarily mobile face summed up expressions of the most diverse feelings, even the "death mask" of Japanese theatre. She started to pose for Rodin the following year. "Her muscles are clearly outlined and stand out like those of the small dogs called fox terriers. Her tendons are so strong that the articulations they are attached to are of the same size as the limbs themselves. She is so robust

[13] This is exactly the opposite of the common inspiration that he himself criticised shortly before passing away: "After the plagiarism of the Greeks and Middle Ages, here come the looters of the Japanese and the Persians. Nothing personal, only weakness." (Marin L.,

"L'éducation d'Art industriel: Le maître Auguste Rodin et l'art industriel appliqué". *L'Œuvre économique*, 25 March 1917, p. 181).

[14] Rodin A., *op. cit.*, 1911, p. 152.

[15] Bourdon G., "Rodin et les petites princesses jaunes", *Le Figaro*, 1st August 1906.

[16] Rodin A., *op. cit.*, 1914, p. 121.

[17] *Idem.*

53 - Auguste Rodin,
**THE ANGEL ON THE SUN DIAL
OF THE CHARTRES CATHEDRAL
NOTED BY RODIN AS HAVING « FOUND
ITS MATCH IN CAMBODIA »,**
graphite on a botebook page, 1906,
D.7044, notebook 50, f°15 v°.

54 - Eduard Steichen,
MASK OF HANAKO,
platinotype, Ph.1019.

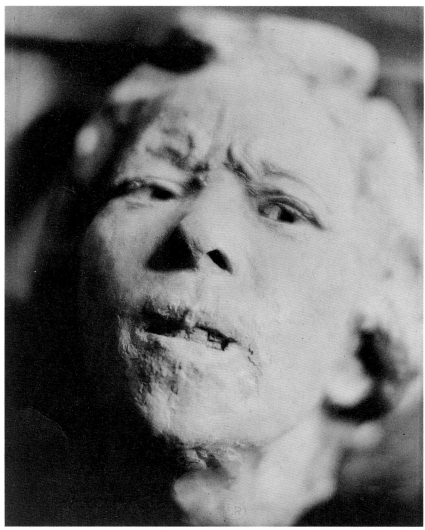

that she can stand for as long as she likes on one leg, with the other raised in front of her at a right angle. […] Her anatomy is therefore quite different from that of European women"[18]. It is not so much this astonishing body as her features that he captures in a series of fifty-three sculpted portraits, with a realism that is sometimes close to being morbid *(fig. 54)*. On the alert for the slightest sign of life, Rodin was stupefied: "When she remained still she preserved her attitude so immobile that it was only the movement of the blood vessels, the trembling of the nostrils that gave a sign of life."[19]. Hanako was a challenge.

55 - Auguste Rodin,
NIJINSKY,
plaster, 1912, S.1185.

The sculptor always attached great importance to studying the expression of feelings. Well before his encounter with the Far East, it had led him, with the same curiosity, first towards the portrait, and then, at the turn of the century, towards dance, which was precisely at the crossroads of his research on movement and inner expression. Observation, certainly, but it was still necessary to go and see for himself. From the veils of Loie Fuller to the extreme sobriety of Isadora Duncan, from the bourrée to the flamenco, from the unthinkable articulation of Nijinsky's body *(fig. 55)* in his performance of *Après-Midi d'un Faune* in 1912 to the suppleness of Alda Moreno at the Opéra Comique, Rodin was unfailingly fascinated. The freedom of his *Dance Movements*, with their pure and almost abstract lines, which he modelled for himself around 1910, are now only traces, signs, essences *(fig. 56)*. Merely because "Understanding means not dying!"[20]

18 Rodin A., *op. cit.*, 1911, p. 152.

19 Rodin A., "Every country has its beautiful women, says Rodin". This cut-out article without any references, is in the archives of the Rodin Museum.

20 Coquiot G., *op. cit.*, 1913, p. 225.

RIGHT PAGE

56 - Auguste Rodin,
DANCE MOVEMENT H,
terracotta, circa 1911, S.118.

NEXT DOUBLE PAGE

Henri Baudoin,
**RODIN AND LOÏE FULLER
IN A RICKSHAW AT THE COLONIAL
EXHIBITION IN MARSEILLES,**
gelatin silver print, July 1906,
Ph.198.

After 1900, when the fame earned by his *Balzac* and his large-scale personal exhibition left him little freedom, and when invitations and exhibitions entailed frequent travels outside France, where unexpected success awaited him, Rodin was still capable of isolating himself to discover the wonders of museums. Although he asked John Marshall, who received him in Rome in 1912, to "show me the small things I don't know" [21], he remained faithful to the Greek marbles in the British Museum of London which, despite being familiar to him, still stirred him with wonder, even at the age of seventy three. Those were always the final lesson. [22]

Even in Paris at the height of his fame, while visiting galleries aimlessly, his attention was caught by a statuette by Maillol, which prompted him to remark: "Do you know why it is so beautiful and why can we spend hours looking at it? It is because it does not try to arouse our curiosity." [23] This was the driving force behind Rodin. He wanted to understand the natural, the perfect expression of the natural in all its paradoxes. He was curious about the visibility of the obvious, or rather, rendering it visible. He was indifferent to all that disturbed or clashed and, consequently, "aroused curiosity". He was fascinated by the Other, starting with woman, the object of endless investigations, as of 1890, down to the most intimate detail.

Talking of the Cubists, revealed at the Salon des Indépendants in 1911, he told the press, who were surprised by his silence: "I have never seen their works and have no wish to do so. I think they are mistaken, one cannot move away from the eternal lessons of nature with impunity. I compare them to the tiny noises of the street. They are discordant notes, the wind will sweep them away!" [24] It is true that Rodin hated noise [25]. He therefore arrogantly ignored the Cubists, Fauvists and other Futurists. This profound incomprehension, at the turning point of two centuries, turned him not so much into the first of the moderns, as people have always wanted to perceive him, but in the final analysis, as perhaps the last of the great classics. Or, to put it in his own words, one of the "penuttimanes" [26]: "I stepped back, and this is how I came to be of the future". [27]

21 Grunfeld F.V., *op. cit.,* 1988, p. 649.

22 "What is the point of going to the British to feel disgusted by all that we make?" (Notebook n° 49, 2nd inner cover, 1913?, Rodin Museum).

23 Rewald J., *Maillol,* Paris, 1939, p. 13; cf. Grunfeld F.V., *op. cit.,* 1988, p. 479.

24 Plessis P., " Sur le boulevard : Quand Rodin descend de l'Olympe ", *L'Intransigeant,* 30 December 1912.

25 "A door that slammed too hard, an object that fell, a sudden footstep, would make him jump. A convulsed expression would spread over his face, his wrinkles would furrow, and his azure eyes would blaze with anger. He could not bear noisy instruments either. Bugles and

trumpets made him ill, nervous and anguished." (Meunier M., "Rodin et la musique", *Revue Pleyel,* n° 18, March 1925).

26 Rodin, quoted by Ludovici A., *Personal Reminiscences of Auguste Rodin,* London, John Murray, 1926, p. 68.

27 Notebook n° 105, f°14 r, before December 1913, Rodin Museum.

my stifling heart …

SECRETIVE

"From time to time, he pulled a sweet out of his pocket and munched it. Then his face became immutable. Under his thick widely arched eyebrows, his ultramarine eyes stared behind a crystal pince-nez. The predominant pyramid of his nose was set between pinkish cheekbones. Only his beard, white, flowing and tipped with amber, swayed majestically in the wind. The left hand, in a grey glove, leaning on his umbrella, fidgeted and stretched as if uncomfortable in its envelope. The right hand, with bare fingers that were powerful at the base, a bit thick at the joints, and square at the tips, was still." [1]

Walter Henry Barnett,
PORTRAIT OF RODIN WITH A PINCE-NEZ,
carbon print, 12 January 1904,
Ph.1094.

Most of his secrets had names, mainly those of his mistresses or members of his family, the one from which he came from and the one he refused to found, despite the birth of a son. These relations were marked by feelings, weakness or fear, self-doubt and pain, which his naturally taciturn and secretive nature refused to disclose. Carried away by his work and career, there was little room in his life for anything else except his sculpture. And of the facts, encounters and sufferings he had hidden, seemingly forced into oblivion by silence, all that remains are his legendary love affair with Camille Claudel, his letters and the profusion of intimate outpourings in his notebooks. Mixed with comments on his travels and sketches of what he observed, they allow an inquisitive reader to penetrate into what were probably the most secret depths of Rodin. These notes were written at an age when memories flooded back to haunt him when he least expected them, when he was unable to withhold expressing his feelings or when the waiting and pain were too strong to be contained.

Rodin seemed to stand alone despite the fact that were too many people around him. But this deep solitude was not of his own choosing. He had always experienced it. His worldly relations, his efforts to organise a career that had taken up more than half of his life, as well as the interminable flow of visits and solicitations – the price of glory – made this solitude all the more precious. It had become his sole refuge, and he turned it into his sole resource.

From his first studio in Rue Lebrun, still close to the family apartment, he gradually moved away from the centre of the capital [2]. He moved as far as Meudon where he

57 - Anonymous,
THE VILLA DES BRILLANTS IN MEUDON,
albumen print, 1893, Ph.1278.

LEFT PAGE

Jean-Baptiste Barnouvin,
PORTRAIT OF MARIA RODIN,
oil on canvas, P.7264.

Anonymous,
MASK OF CAMILLE CLAUDEL ON A STAND,
printing-out paper, circa 1900, Ph.1964.

Anonymous,
RODIN IN HIS DINING ROOM IN MEUDON,
aristotype, Ph.263.

Anonymous,
INTERIOR OF THE FOLIE NEUFBOURG,
printing-out paper, 1910, Ph.1183.

1 Georges-Michel M., *Peintres et sculpteurs que j'ai connus,* New York, Brentano's, 1942, p. 262.

2 "Rodin's studio was a mysterious retreat, situated in an out-of-the-way spot in the town. It even seems as if the creation of each of the works that tormented him required a different kind of solitude. He thus set a rendez-vous with himself, at the Faubourg Saint-Jacques, another time at Boulevard de Vaugirard. He worked there in contemplation and silence, assuming an unsociable coyness in concealing his happiness at creating in distant districts, and even more unknown than distant." (Maillard L., *op. cit.,* 1899, p. 22).

58 - Anonymous,
**LA FOLIE NEUFBOURG AT CLOS PAYEN,
VIEWED FROM THE BOULEVARD D'ITALIE**
Postcard, 1910.

59 - Camille Claudel to Rodin,
« MONSIEUR RODIN... » (DETAIL),
from Islette, summer 1890 or 1891.
Ma.102

settled with Rose in 1893 [3] *(fig. 57).* He finally bought the Villa des Brillants two years later. He started in working-class districts, at 117 Boulevard de Vaugirard, where he worked on *The Burghers of Calais* in 1886. Then came the dilapidated house of the Folie Neufbourg, at 68 Boulevard d'Italie [4], which sheltered his love and work with Camille Claudel *(fig. 58),* for whom he rented a studio almost opposite, at number 113. This was a secret and forbidden studio where nobody was allowed to come. He regretfully left it in 1898 at the same time as Camille who abandoned hers to move to Rue de Turenne. Was this a first separation, six years before the one that led him to Meudon in 1893, far from the demanding life of the capital. "He said he was unwell and suffering from a neuralgia that prevented him from sleeping. He had aged: his clear complexion was blotched with dark patches; under his reddened eyelids, his eyes had a worried and anxious look; he no longer smiled, his tense features expressed an unhealthy obsession. He alluded to serious problems, and his shoulders seemed to shrug off their burden with unconscious movements. He seemed to be going through one of the most tormented phases of his life. […] For the health of his wife and for his own, he claimed, he was now obliged to live in the country." [5]

Camille Claudel, who was 24 years his junior, appeared Rodin's life in 1883 and in his studio the following year. The student, with her "superb forehead over magnificent eyes of a dark blue rarely found except in a novel" [6], inspired an intense passion, and the surviving letters tell of overwhelming and desperate torments. She was talented, she sculpted the hands and feet of Rodin's figures, and their sculpture reached such a degree of fusion that it sometimes sets off controversies over attribution even now. Although Rodin introduced Miss Claudel as "my student", Camille herself remained secretive. She was Mademoiselle Say, a coded nickname for the witnesses of their relationship or CCC, simple initials in his notebooks that sometimes give a glimpse of the pain of absence, like these disjointed words in which Camille inevitably incarnates suffering: "As in the past you today torn pain […] CCC. I look upon you as a divine woman. Do you prefer that I am incapable of rendering the extraordinary

3 They then moved into a house known as "Chien-Loup" which Léon Maillard described: "in the upper rooms, on the furniture, on the tables, on the chests, were rough shapes, minor indications, groups more clearly formulated, figures, pieces abruptly detached from an ensemble that did not satisfy him, and here and there, an antique head, a sculpted Medieval piece, a Greek urn." (Maillard L., *op. cit.,* 1899, p. 39).

4 The present Boulevard Blanqui.

5 Cladel J., *op. cit.,* 1936, pp. 42-43.

6 Claudel P., "Camille Claudel", *Camille Claudel,* Rodin Museum exhibition catalogue, November-December 1951, p. 3.

7 Notebook n° 42, f°83 r° and v°, between January and March 1913, Rodin Museum.

8 Notebook n° 40, f°40 v°, around 1911 ?, Rodin Museum.

60 - Camille Claudel,
MATURITY, SECOND VERSION,
bronze, 1898, S.1380.

61 - Anonymous,
**RODIN AND ROSE BEURET IN THE GARDEN
OF MEUDON,**
gelatin silver print, 25 March 1916,
Ph.1105.

side your gentleness is here beside my studies. You are near my studies, divine character you exalt me"[7] *(fig. 59)*. For this is what it really was all about, the emulation of two artists in a destructive passion, that Camille's jealousy, a forewarning of her persecution mania, rendered even more fragile. This is illustrated in the drawings of 1893, sent to Rodin, portraying him bound to Rose, or *Maturity (fig. 60),* with its explicit autobiographical references. In 1906, Camille cut herself off from the world and started the process of self-destruction that would end up in her being confined to a mental hospital in 1913.

Unfortunately for Camille, as he wrote in a notebook, "a man who has loved a woman goes back to her with the ardour of his soul and not of his body"[8]. Rodin had that fidelity "of the soul". That woman, who he would only legitimately marry a few days before she died, was Rose, "a good companion who I am always happy to return to"[9] *(fig. 61)*. And although he could not help treating her with extreme indifference, and sometimes with brutality[10], even in front of visitors at Meudon where she cloistered herself, he always went back to her[11]. More than neglected, Rose was deliberately kept away from Rodin's professional life, and her self-denial bordered on the sacrifice. There is no doubt that she fulfilled perfectly the expectations of the sculptor who on several occasions could not help saying, "She is attached to me like an animal"[12].

9 Cladel J., *op. cit.*, 1903, p. 109.

10 "[…] I do everything to ensure that Monsieur Rodin does not glare at me with his terrible look. When he is angry, the way he looks frightens me. His hard look is a real despair for me. I have never, in the thirty years or more that we have lived together, been able to get used to it. […] I don't accompany him on his visits either; he receives people who are too grand and chic for me. When they come to see him, I prefer to go down to my pantry." (Rose Beuret, quoted by Meunier M., *op. cit.*, 21 September 1918).

11 I have loved women other than mine, but I never left her." (Rodin, quoted by Cladel J., *op. cit.*, 1936, p. 234).

12 A confidence noted in the diary of Victoria Sackville-West, 14 March 1914, private collection (cf. Grunfeld F.V., *op. cit.*, 1988, p. 56).

"I like obedient women"[13]. "With my wife, I can think because she consents in advance and without disturbing me. I know she is enjoying herself." [14]. He even emphasised an outstanding feature of her character to Dujardin-Beaumetz, when he said she was "always ready to devote herself to me; this is what she has done all her life." [15] She was proud to serve the sculptor [16].

Was this because he had nothing better? ... Visitors were sometimes surprised to learn that this woman, who addressed him formally and did not always sit at table, was his companion. Rainer Maria Rilke saw how remote Rodin was from everyday life, except when he was sculpting. "[…] his house and the noises of the house were so indescribably infinite and secondary that one had the impression of seeing it only in a dream, with strange gaps and an entire range of faded memories. His daily life and the people who belonged to it seemed liked an empty bed where it had ceased to flow; but there was nothing sad about this; nearby, one could hear the rumbling, the powerful sound of the river that had no wish to split into two arms …" [17]

Rilke may have been right, and if so, Rose Beuret may not even have been a secret. If she was not actually absent from his life, she was simply present in the shadow, more like an asexual mother than a woman. Becoming aware, with age, of the force of her devotion, he finally understood [18]. And rather than finding excuses for her being unsociable ("She is shy") [19], after fifty years of infidelities, he swore to be faithful to her on 29 January 1917 by giving her his name two weeks before she died. At that point, while she was dying, he made an ultimate confession that she was no longer able to hear: "what an indefinable end, the plans were always immense and here is the result, she has stripped things down to basics, she has breathed air into things, into lives, mine" [20]. Contemplating her body, he came back, despite himself, to what had been all his life, a final image that superimposed itself on Rose, before covering her again: "She is beautiful. This is sculpture, this is quite clearly sculpture." [21] *(fig. 62)*. Even though Gustave Coquiot knew Rodin well, he dared to write in the same year: "He loves sculpture so much that it has taken everything from him, heart and mind. Not one of us can flatter ourselves by claiming to have had even a brief friendship with such a man; it does not exist." [22] And there lies, unquestionably, the key to his success.

[13] Tirel M., *op. cit.*, 1923, p. 36.

[14] Notes and Drafts, VII-A4a, Rodin Museum.

[15] Dujardin-Beaumetz H., *op. cit.*, 1913, p. 117.

[16] "My entire concern is to look after him well, and I assure you I have enough to do to please Monsieur Rodin. I make sure his dinner is served on time, that his eggs are well done. Every evening, when he returns, he finds a bowl of warm milk and his slippers by the fireplace. I am happy when Monsieur Rodin is satisfied." (Rose Beuret, quoted by Meunier M., *op. cit.*, 21 September 1918).

[17] Rilke R.M., Letter to Lou Andreas-Salomé, Oberneuland, near Bremen, 8 August 1903, *op. cit.*, 1976, p. 32.

[18] "I am no longer as impatient and despotic as before, and how sure I was that everone did not suffer because of what was natural to me. My poor wife will be my heart, my well cared for princess. " (Notes and Drafts, XB-41, Rodin Museum).

[19] To the novelist Léon Cladel, in Cladel J., *op. cit.*, 1936, p. 34.

Rodin had never wanted to start a family. It was his friends who organised the unexpected marriage for inheritance reasons. His son Auguste, born in 1866, two years after he met Rose - of an unknown father according to his birth certificate - always bore his mother's name. The silence around him was heavy, the rejection total, as if he were a hindrance to his father's career, something shameful that had to be hidden. A "good for nothing", undisciplined and "irresponsible", as Rodin described him. His aunt Thérèse had difficulty in bringing him up while his parents were in Belgium in the 1870s. He apparently fell from the second floor apartment and had become mentally deficient. No one knows what really happened. Only Thérèse knew. And yet the Rodin family had its share of

misfortunes. The father, Jean-Baptiste, and two aunts suffered from mental disorders, the latter seriously enough to be confined to a mental hospital. A half-sister, Clotilde, stands out by her absence. [23] A heavy family heritage enclosed by a wall of silence.

Rodin nonetheless tried to inculcate in his son a work ethic and discipline in drawing and engraving, as his own father had done before him. In 1879, he reminded Rose, "Tell Auguste that I would like him to be good. Give him some paper and try to make him work and fill in 15 exercise books for me, and make men on horseback" [24]. Over time, Rodin's relationship with him was reduced exclusively to financial matters. It took the outbreak of war in 1914 for Rodin to bring his son from the heights of Saint-Ouen where he lived in poverty, close to him in Meudon, as a final recognition, like a confession. [25] It was only late in life that Rodin, overcome by remorse and troubled by his ingratitude, felt a need to prove once again that he was grateful to those close to him who he had frequently forgotten or neglected in a career that nothing could hinder. He became aware of the important role of these intimate stages in his life when he was old and memories rushed back to him. Was he thinking of Auguste Beuret when he wrote, "At the end of one's life, there are acts to be judged, this, perhaps, is the Last Judgement. We feel some regret over our ingratitude and major faults that sometimes persisted throughout a lifetime" [26] *(fig. 63)*.

20 Notes and Drafts, IIIDa-1, Rodin Museum.

21 Cladel J., *op. cit.*, 1936, p. 396.

22 Coquiot G., *op. cit.*, 1917, p. 33.

23 Thérèse is the only person who mentioned her as the bad reference in relation to the young Auguste, Thérèse Cheffer to Rodin, 19 August 1873, Ma. 2564, Rodin museum.

24 Rodin to Rose Beuret, [Nice, after 10 August 1879], L. 15, Rodin

Museum.

25 Edmond Beuret, Rose's nephew, who had been asked by Rodin to persuade Auguste, nevertheless states: "They will therefore come here under the name of Mr. and Mrs. Menier. Mr. Menier will be an engraver working for Monsieur Rodin and will at the same time guard his property. In this way, the matter is clear and no one will really know who they are. There will therefore be no gossip and no problems for you." (Letter to Rodin at Châtelet-en-Brie, Paris, 77 rue de

Varenne, 27 July 1914, Ma. 2578, Rodin Museum).

26 Notes and Drafts, XBa-5, Rodin Museum.

Rodin had two sisters and a brother. He never talked about Anna Olympie, the younger sister. He was only eight years old when she died. His brother, Angelo Stanislas Constantin, was born a few months later, and even though he was his godson at his christening in the church of Saint Médard on 26 May 1848, he was always a blank in the story of his life[27]. Today, this strange silence can only prompt questions. Only traces of the existence of Maria, the older sister, have survived. She loved her younger brother. Being very determined and influential, she was able to persuade her parents to show confidence in the young Auguste whose vocation was beginning to blossom. On the other hand, she made him feel guilty when he decided to leave the family home in 1861. In the end, she was the one who abandoned them all by joining an order of nuns in the autumn of the same year. Her brother was so devastated by her death, only a few months after she took her vows, that he joined a religious congregation at 68 rue du Faubourg Saint-Jacques. He became an Augustinian brother before realising, while sculpting the bust of Father Eymard, the head of the congregation, that his real vocation did not lie within those walls *(fig. 64)*. The memory of Maria did not erase his passion for sculpture.

His father was spared from oblivion *(fig. 65)*. He had a strong image and played a role model despite the mental disorder, coupled with an increasing blindness, which led to his early retirement. When he was far away in Belgium, as of 1871, Rodin worried about him. "Go and see father, tell me how he is"[28], he wrote to Rose who had remained in Paris. In 1877, she returned from Belgium, where she had joined Rodin, and took over from Aunt Thérèse[29], caring for him with her usual sense of devotion until he died in 1883. This was the period of *Bellone*. Rose's features were already hardened. Is it because Rodin had become fickle? All his life, Rodin felt a great respect towards his father. To this was added his gratitude for his father's active support and the confidence he showed in him, despite his failure to be admitted to the Ecole des Beaux-Arts. According to one of his secretaries "he remained silent for a long time when he was told about it". He inherited his determination and obstinacy from his father.

Little is know about his mother, an extremely pious and self-effacing woman *(fig. 66)*. However, a few personal notes written when he was old reveal his gratitude: "The enchantment of loving my mother who gave me her soul while forming it. [...] she was all reason. She was duty with good education, with infinite smiles. She was as

64 - Charles Aubry,
RODIN WORKING ON THE BUST OF FATHER EYMARD,
albumen print, 1863, Ph.158.

[27] Baptism certificate of the parish of Saint Médard, D. 6J.2855, f°97, Archives of Paris.

[28] Rodin to Rose Beuret, [Brussels, 1st October 1871], L. 5, Rodin Museum.

[29] The solution found until then, on the suggestion of Auguste Cheffer, a first cousin, was "to have my uncle [Jean-Baptiste] and the young one [Auguste] live with my mother [Thérèse] and my aunt, this does not seem to displease him, in that way he will never be on his own and will always be warm, two important aspects for him." (Letter from Auguste Cheffer to Rodin, Paris, 20 November 1871, Ma. 2563, Rodin Museum).

noble as a duchess. What order! She died in the belief that none of her qualities were in me, for the triumph of her character had not yet been revealed to her. Her strong character re-emerged in me. With her protective eyes, she made me yield to her. Thanks be given to the woman who gave me all my talents, who loved me with a genuine love, the life she made so beautiful for me …What a rich harvest from an intelligent woman!" "For I was brought up by a pious mother; she turned me into an artist without knowing it. She did not like them. Artistic disorder". "I set off to wander through the memories of my childhood, my mother my sister accompanied me my despair made me …"[30] One last word, almost illegible (can one dare to read the word *pray*?), marks the silent grief of losing these two women, a suffering that would affect all Rodin's future relations with women. In addition to the responsibility of his future, should one also blame his mother for not being able to build anything besides his career at the same time?

In 1879, for instance, he wrote to Rose: "it is astonishing how expansive I can be when I am away from you"[31]. Only distance, in space or in time, enabled Rodin to allow his feelings, his emotions or his fears to well up. With old age, during the moments of solitude he set aside to "mature his soul"[32], he started to feel the first stirrings of anguish, no doubt due to his inactivity. And with it came the time to review his life: "Desperate me – cruel moment, I feel death before it comes. These moments of waiting for death (corridor) my enthusiasm is dead, I notice beauty without it penetrating me, I am now excluded, and all this overcomes my heart which is stifling, life made me bad"[33] *(fig. 66 bis)*. And because all his life was given to sculpture, when it abandoned him, he admitted with these few – and final – words, "I do not like myself." [34]

65 - Auguste Rodin,
PORTRAIT OF JEAN-BAPTISTE, HIS FATHER,
oil on canvas, 1863, P.7247.

66 - Pierre Eugène Thiebault,
PORTRAIT OF MARIE RODIN,
THE SCULPTOR'S MOTHER,
albumen paper, before 1871, Ph.1.

66 bis - *Paris Soir*,
ARTICLE OF 28 MAY 1930.

[30] Successively : Notes and Drafts, XBa-40, Notes and Drafts, VIIA4a, Rodin Museum, Notebook n° 88, f°20 r°, before 1914, Rodin Museum.

[31] Rodin to Rose Beuret, [Strasbourg, autumn 1879], L. 16, Rodin Museum.

[32] Rodin to Hélène de Nostitz, [Paris or Meudon, July 1908], L. 828, Rodin Museum.

[33] Notebook n° 71, f°14 v°, Rodin Museum.

[34] Notebook n°97, f°12 v°, Rodin Museum.

one must unfreeze sculpture …

BOLD

"The man, he is in front of you, his clothes stained with plaster, his hands sticky with clay. He is small, stocky and quiet. All his facial features appear at the same time because they are all characteristic. Between hair cut very short and a long blond beard flowing down to his chest, a fine face, changing from distracted to anxious and from anxious to smiling, is veiled by preoccupations and lights up with peaceful joy and silent kindness. The forehead, a little mystical and vaguely ogival, but very broad and well rounded, is made to enclose and seal numerous thoughts. The straight nose completes a profile similar to the profiles of monks sculpted on cathedral portals. But this benevolent and subtle monk is armed with a critical spirit and determination, and in his artist's cell he is haunted not only by worries but also by modern certainties. His expression and his voice are of a rare harmony, a sharp and brilliant look that combines light and the pale blue colour of his eyes, a soft, intimate and penetrating voice with a good-natured wonder and caustic hint constantly present in his laughter."[1]

Paris, Place de l'Alma. An immaculate pavilion sprang up in a few months in the midst of the chestnut trees. Above the rotunda of the entrance, two words with capital letters: "Rodin Exhibition". The year is 1900 and Rodin had used all the means at his disposal for his first personal exhibition in France. On the fringe of the Universal Exhibition (no less!), he presented all his works in a pavilion he had built at his own expense *(figs. 67 and 68)*. It was a retrospective of the kind usually reserved for artists who are dead, as the press pointed out critically. Yet the artist was very much

[1] Geffroy G., "Le statuaire Rodin", *Les Lettres et les Arts,* Paris, September 1889, p. 291.

Anonymous,
**PORTRAIT OF RODIN
WITH TOUSLED HAIR,**
gelatin silver print, 1907,
Ph.774.

LEFT PAGE

Anonymous,
**RODIN LEANING ON THE MONUMENT
TO VICTOR HUGO
IN THE ALMA PAVILION,**
printing-out paper, Ph.75.

Stephen Haweis et Henry Coles,
**BUSTE OF VICTOR HUGO
AND TWO MEDITATIONS,**
biochromate-gum print ?
1903-1904, Ph.965.

Auguste Rodin,
LAND AND SEA,
plaster on a pink-patinated plinth,
1900 ? S.5704.

Auguste Rodin,
**ASSEMBLAGE : TWO EVES
AND THE CROUCHING WOMAN,**
plaster and branches,
circa 1905-1907, S.184.

Auguste Rodin,
THE CREATION,
terracotta, circa 1890-1900 ?
S.266.

67 - E. Bauche,
**EXTERIOR OF THE RODIN
EXHIBITION PAVILION,
PLACE DE L'ALMA IN PARIS,**
printing-out paper, 1900, Ph.1375.

68 - Eugène Carrière,
**POSTER FOR THE RODIN EXHIBITION,
PARIS, PLACE DE L'ALMA, 1900,**
Af. 106-1.

alive, and very often in his pavilion, waiting for clients, who did not flock to the exhibition in large numbers. And for the occasion, he adopted the attitude of a teacher: "[…] it is the first time I have undertaken to assemble all my works together and submit them to the public. Unfortunately, the artistic education of this public has been so distorted by exhibitions of an official, industrial and absurd art that I fear I will not be understood immediately by the crowd. The goal I am pursuing, therefore, is to set right and extol the sense of art in a public that is more capable than imagined of assimilating simple and forceful aesthetics. My pretensions will no doubt be considered rather arrogant, but I am convinced that by showing "my sculpture" and how I perceive sculpture, I will render a service to the cause of art." [2] Rodin hoped he had the power of persuasion. Admittedly, he was already sixty years old and did not have much to lose …

As the perfect way to stage his work, he dared to make an extreme use of white. He displayed his plasters in the light, permanently, with contrasts created by a few bronzes and the leaves of the chestnut trees outlined in the windows, "natural frescoes" as he liked to call them.[3] What was important was to put the result of all his research on display. First of all, his research on light, which had reached its culminating point with the *Balzac*, exhibited under the gibes of the crowds two years earlier: "[…] this building is a unique, incomparable and spacious place, leaving all the room necessary to stand back, so perfectly lit that not one point of a work is in the shadow, it is the open air and it i. a shelter." [4] And secondly, his research on space, which he insisted should surround his sculptures: "A sculpture must have its own atmosphere around it, a certain space enabling a visitor to examine it under various aspects." [5]

Pierre de Wissant, headless and armless, visible from the street, welcomed visitors in the rotunda. *Balzac* stood in the axis. The tone was set, the exhibition would make no concessions. More than putting himself in the limelight, Rodin, in all sincerity, actually opened himself to attack. In fact, *The Gates of Hell*, the linchpin of the exhibition, had been relegated to the side, even though everyone was impatient to see it. The press had for several years been waiting eagerly for its completion, the "great work of Monsieur Rodin", which had started to cost a lot of money to the State and which at long last was to be shown to the public. But it was empty. Rodin had dismantled the figures that had given life to the door leaves. According to *L'Art Décoratif*, since they were of a darker shade, they did not match the whiteness of the plaster [6]. In the final analysis, however, the reason was not important. Only *The Shades* perched at the top indicated, by the triangle of their arms, the power and absurdity of this situation. A closed *Door* then, and what is more, it no longer had value as a backing for sculpture, or not yet. It was a

2 Rodin, quoted by Schneider G., "L'exposition privée de Rodin", *Le Petit Bleu de Paris*, 19 July 1899.

3 Grautoff O., "Bei Rodin", *Kunst und Künstler*, October 1904, p. 4.

4 Rodin, quoted in "Rodin sur le pavé", *Le Petit Bleu de Paris*, 20 December 1900.

5 Rodin, quoted by Schneider G., *loc. cit.*

6 Anonymous, *L'Art Décoratif*, June 1900.

pure work of art, almost an abstraction, a
structure, Anatole France was convinced of this:
"In the state it is in at present, cast in plaster, its
leaves shorn of the figures in high relief that were
supposed to be applied to them, it is a work with
a deep meaning and powerful expression. I do
not know of anything more pathetic."[7]. In light
and space, between architecture and sculpture,
the empty *Gates* were not completely
incongruous, it was simply a hybrid among
hybrids *(fig. 69)*.

The *Gates* were finally on display, a clamorous
symbol, a temporal dimension of the work,
accompanied by a host of studies[8] that the
public and critics, accustomed to the sculptor's
whims but unable to understand, ended up by
accepting, if not actually expecting. For of course
in Rodin's view, an exhibition did not imply
completion. Nothing, he felt, could stop an
evolution, for this was in the very nature of a
work of art. And it was this aspect that he
wanted to show as it was precisely because of
this ever-changing nature that art deserved its
name. In this sense, plaster, usually a temporary
material, an invisible phase in the path towards

a bronze or marble, without being an end in itself, had a life of its own. The casts of
his terracotta and plaster works, far from being restricted to the standard and
indispensable process of making a bronze, were an invitation to systematically explore
the possibilities of multiple variations. The great innovation introduced by Rodin was
in the co-existence of phases that, in keeping with tradition, should normally succeed
each other in time. However, for him, every phase, every transformation, left a trace,
leading systematically to one − or several − casts of the same work[9]. And each one of
them acquired a unique character through alteration, addition or fragmentation, thus
reviving the immediate relevance of creation.

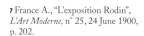

69 · Eugène Druet,
**THE GATES OF HELL
IN THE ALMA PAVILION,**
gelatin silver print, 1900,
Ph.285.

7 France A., "L'exposition Rodin",
L'Art Moderne, n° 25, 24 June 1900,
p. 202.

8 "From the period of *The Gates of
Hell*, Rodin started to describe as
works his fragments, his studies.
[...] He was more satisfied with
those of his partial studies that
seemed to be successful than
certain small works that were
completely finished." (Kahn G.,
Silhouettes littéraires, Paris, published
by Montaigne, 1925, p. 88).

9 "When he thinks he has found it,
he has it cast, starts all over again,
makes another cast. These are
approximations that will result in a
final formula." *(idem).*

RIGHT PAGE

71 - Jacques-Ernest Bulloz,
**THE GREAT SHADE IN THE GARDEN
OF MEUDON,**
gelatin silver print, Ph.302

70 - Auguste Rodin,
ASSEMBLAGE : TWO STUDIES FOR IRIS,
patinated plaster,
circa 1908-1909 ? S.3418.

Naturally, the thinking of an artist is never linear, and Rodin was no exception to this rule. But it was not so much a question of sketches, in the usual sense of the term, but a maximum exploitation of the casting process to multiply the same form, to develop its individuality, before incorporating it – sometimes elsewhere – in various other works *(fig. 70)*. This was perhaps the stance taken by Rodin against industrialisation, which he believed was beginning to reign supreme. And from decentring to displacing, he continuously developed an infinity of variations, with a delight that prevented completion[10]. In everything he undertook from that point onwards, leaving his work in progress in that state had the same importance as the work itself. But the public did not understand his approach; it confused the unfinished with the incomplete, and perceived it as a provocation, a challenge to conformity. Indifferent to the reaction of the critics, Rodin was sure of himself. He set himself as an example and a model, because if he was daring, it was to convince.[11]

The Gates of Hell, amputated of its figures before the exhibition, was a perfect example. By doing this, Rodin made his position as clear as in a letter written in 1897 to Eugene of Sweden on the subject of his fragmentary *Meditation*: "[…] the study of Nature is complete in it and I have made every effort to render art as whole as possible. I consider this plaster to be one of my most finished works, the most advanced. […] As it is – fragmentary and in plaster – it will be displayed in the Museum of Marseilles"[12]. Rodin used all the arguments he could think of and even added the somewhat hackneyed one about the "lesson of the antique". In the end, *The Walking Man* sold rather well.

As for Rilke, he was completely won over. Living with Rodin had given him the keys: "[…] the arms are missing. In this case, Rodin felt they were too easy a solution for his task, like something that did not match the body, which wanted to be wrapped in itself, without outside assistance. One can think of Eleonora Duse, in a drama by d'Annunzio, who painfully abandoned, tries to embrace without arms and to hold without hands. This scene […] conveyed the impression that arms were a luxury, an ornament, a stroke of luck for the rich and overindulgent, that one could throw far away to become completely poor. She did not seem to have sacrificed anything important; […] The same applies to Rodin's statues without arms; nothing necessary is missing. One stands before them as if they were whole, finished, and rejecting any complement."[13] These fragmented and enlarged figures *(fig. 71)*, in all their variations, appeared very early, shortly after 1880, the year when the *Gates* were commissioned, as if it were finally an unexpected pretext to set in motion a system that would reach its peak about ten years

10 See Didi-Huberman G., " Figée à son insu dans un moule magique … Anachronisme du moulage, histoire de la sculpture, archéologie de la modernité", *Les Cahiers du musée National d'art moderne*, n° 54, Winter 1995, pp. 81-113.

11 For details about the Rodin exhibition at Place de l'Alma in 1900, see *Rodin en 1900*, exhibition catalogue, Luxembourg Museum, 12 March-15 July 2001, Paris, Rodin Museum-Réunion des Musées Nationaux Publications, 2001.

12 Rodin to Eugene of Sweden, Paris, 2 January 1897, Prins Eugens Waldemarsudde, Stockholm.

13 Rilke R.M., *Auguste Rodin*, Paris, Emile-Paul Frères, 1928, pp. 52-53.

72 - Eugène Druet,
**THE MONUMENT TO VICTOR HUGO
AT THE SALON OF 1897,**
gelatin silver print, April-June 1897,
Ph.1950.

later. What ensued was pure research based on possible settings for the *Gates,* calling for an interaction between the figures, after they were extracted, isolated and perfected individually. Gradually, caught in the net of this system, the assemblages functioned autonomously, outside their original frame.

Another illustration, far removed from the *Gates,* was the second *Monument to Victor Hugo,* commissioned in 1889, which crystallised the same problems and was presented at the Salon of 1897 as a colossal assemblage *(fig. 72).* " 'Arms of a Woman, incomplete' describes the catalogue. It might just as well say 'Incomplete Group', for it is no longer a matter of not being finished, it has hardly been started. The most admirable aspect is that movement has become visible. And this movement is superb. But is this Mr. Rodin's only gift?" [14] In fact, "the right arm of Victor Hugo is stretched out as if to impose silence on all voices that might disturb his own inner voices. However, this arm was cut off, sawn off, raised several centimetres; two plaster links attached it to the shoulder, two brackets supported it, but the connection was not made and an angular hollow remained under the armpit", observed Jeanès.[15] The enlarged *Tragic Muse* (with a hollow in the left arm) was arranged on a wood scaffolding, and the *Inner Voice* placed just behind it. Since the general composition broke away radically from the traditionally imposed pyramid for public monuments, two of the inspiring muses had to be eliminated. The two remaining muses were no longer restricted to the accessory role of accompanying the principal figure. A play of multiple lines converged towards the poet's head in a perfect equilibrium, creating a unity in the monument through the rhythm of the limbs.

Yet Rodin still had a long way to go before the audacity of the installation that he would set up in 1901-1902 for the *Monument to Puvis de Chavannes,* the venerated painter who had died in 1898. All the components had been made previously: the bust of the artist ten years before, a simple table, a pedestal and a Corinthian capital. The *Spirit of Eternal Repose,* exhibited two years earlier in Belgium, points towards the artist's bust,

14 R.B., "Le Salon du Champ-de-Mars", *Le Moniteur Universel,* 24 April 1897.

15 Jeanès J.E.S., *op. cit.,* 1946, p. 136.

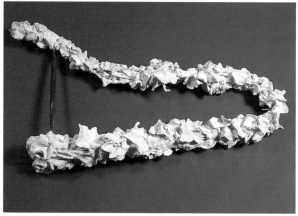

73 - Jean-François Limet ?
**MONUMENT TO PUVIS DE CHAVANNES
IN THE ALMA PAVILION IN MEUDON,**
printing-out paper, circa 1901-1902 ? Ph.384.

74 - Auguste Rodin,
IVY GARLAND FOR THE WHISTLER MUSE,
plaster and wood, after 1912, S.6655.

following the oblique line of the branch of an apple tree cast from life. The effigy of the deceased thus became an accessory, perched on top of a composite pedestal and knitting together the orthogonal lines of the piled up objects *(fig. 73).*

By 1905, it would disappear completely in the last monument commissioned from Rodin, the one dedicated to the painter James Mac Neil Whistler, whom he had replaced the year before as President of the International Society of London. All that remained was a large-scale inspiring muse, the draped version of which was embellished with a garland of ivy leaves dipped in plaster *(fig. 74).* It was a just reversal of the controversy over *The Age of Bronze* that had broken out nearly thirty years earlier. Rodin was now at the height of his glory and no longer hesitated. And as if taking revenge, the model - modest foliage - displayed itself, imprisoned in plaster, as a way of freezing time.

75 - Auguste Rodin,
**ASSEMBLAGE: TORSO OF A WOMAN
IN AN ANTIQUE VASE,**
plaster and pottery, 1895-1900, S.3856.

Rodin would go even further, extending his entrenched position by a dual reflection on the notion of assemblage, introduced at an early stage with the figures of the *Gate,* and the status of the artwork. Far from focusing exclusively on the formal relationship between figures [16], he had no hesitation in assembling them with already existing but unique elements: rough plants with sombre and highly structuring lines, or pieces of old pottery from his personal collection, finally demystified *(fig. 75).* He then gave to his free, whole or fragmented plaster bodies a base in the true sense of the term. He attached them to the ground, arranging them into the simple, manufactured, shape of vases that imposed the angle from which they were viewed.

[16] "Besides many now well-known pieces, he showed me a cupboard full of *maquettes* exquisitely modelled. He would take two or three of these and group them together, first in one way and then in another. They gave him ideas for his compositions, he said." (Rothenstein W., *Men and Memories, 1872–1900,* London, Faber & Faber Ltd., 1931, p. 320).

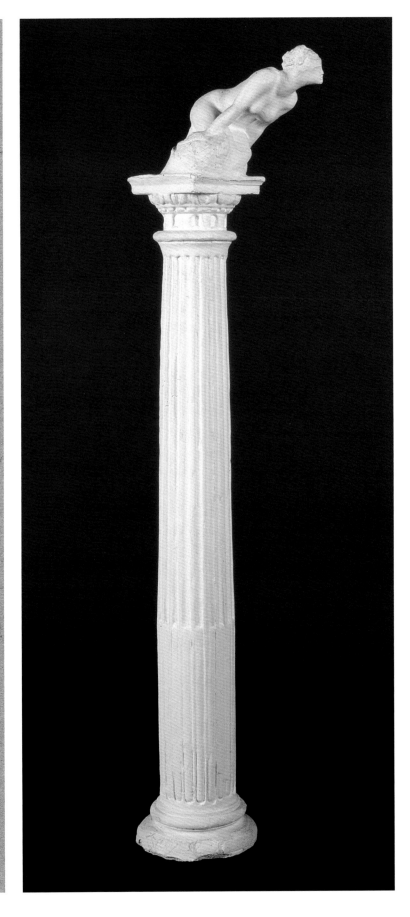

L'ASSIETTE AU BE

Quelque chose de M. Rodin.

77 - **"Quelque chose de M. Rodin"**, (« **Something by Mr. Rodin** »), *L'Assiette au beurre*, special issue, 1900 ?

78 - Auguste Rodin, **Female sphynx on a column**, plaster, 1900, S.2478.

76 - Auguste Rodin, **Draped woman, standing, left profile**, graphite and stump on buff paper, circa 1900, D.1068.

In the same spirit, he stood them on pedestals, leading us to the problem of presentation, at the other end of formal work. The pedestal was always a source of preoccupation for Rodin, even though his research on this question was not always understood *(fig. 77)*. Following the examples in which pottery gradually started to come to terms with the forms, *The Female Sphynx,* exhibited at the Place de l'Alma in 1900, was cast with its column *(figs. 76 and 78)*. The work stood out as its own culminating point, in the same way as *The Hand of God* exhibited vertically, like in Vienna in 1903 *(fig. 79)*, *Iris* standing upright permanently to delimit the distance of respect, and the *Martyr* falling down, once all the stabilising elements were removed *(fig. 80)*.

We are past 1900, far from the first considerations of the place of the viewer in the perception of the work, probably inaugurated by *The Burghers of Calais*. Rodin had wavered between a heroic presentation *(fig. 81)* and an almost non existent pedestal [17], envisaged as early as 1893 but only imposed in 1911 for the monument in London. In this constant consideration for the way his sculpture was viewed, he soon recognised the extraordinary opportunities offered by the technique of photography. Far from using it for documentary purposes, he would turn it into a tool for exploration, a new instrument of research. Just as he kept traces of the phases of his works by making casts, he quickly turned to photography as a means of fixing the ephemeral in certain assemblages *(fig. 82)*. It was a way of preserving the profile of forms already re-transformed,

[17] "[…] I had thought that if placed very low, the group would become more familiar and would involve the public more closely in the pathos and sacrifice, of the drama I would say." (Rodin to Omer Dewavrin, Mayor of Calais, 8 December 1893, Muncipal Archives, Calais). "No pedestal, naïve big man! There is an aesthetic approach to the pedestal at the Beaux-Arts. It is very high, except in gardens for personifications of rivers; probably because their base should appear to be placed on a bank; but for an ordinary statue, the pedestal must be higher than the statue, at least twice as high. It was barely lowered under Louis-Philippe! A concession to prevent the French revolution of 1848. The Second Empire returned abruptly to a very high pedestal. It is difficult to understand Rodin… He comes to a compromise… He accepts a half-pedestal. He is unable to do away with it. If he had been at the Institute, he would have said no pedestal, what a success! "how original!'. So he does not know whether he should console himself for being excluded from commissions in marble or staff" (Kahn G., *op. cit.*, 1925, p. 85).

79 - Anonymous,
**THE HAND OF GOD PRESENTED
IN A PERPENDICULAR POSITION
IN VIENNA IN 1903,**
printing-out paper, Ph.371.

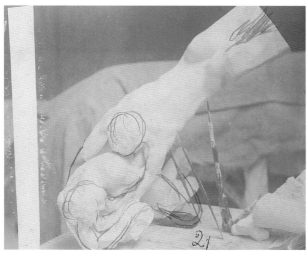

82 - Charles Bodmer,
DAWN,
albumen paper, touched up with graphite
by Rodin, Ph.1056.

80 - Eugène Druet ?
THE MARTYR IN FRONT OF DRAPERY,
gelatin silver print, Ph.306.

RIGHT PAGE

81 - Eugène Druet,
**THE BURGHERS OF CALAIS ON SCAFFOLDING
IN THE GARDEN IN MEUDON,**
gelatin silver print, 1st September 1913,
Ph.1362

already re-used, in order to study its validity. The possibility of multiplying the prints, like the casts of a sculpture, permitted touching up. Graphics could be added to the gelatine silver negative to rework the form in its entirety and simulate other profiles. The photographic image pushed the unfinished work to the brink, but it was an illusion to think it was the last possibility of capturing it.

He worked in close collaboration with his photographers and made exacting demands as to how to view his works, rejecting black grounds to focus on their vibrant edges set against a backdrop [18]. He went as far as to control the distribution of his work. For in this case too, the tool came out of the studio for the viewer, in a concern to teach. Exhibited next to the actual works in Geneva in 1896, their images, controlled and selected by the sculptor, initiated a strange dialogue with the sculptures, and by organising the way they were viewed, they provided the keys to understanding and trained the viewer's perception. And it also justified Rodin's audacity.

[18] "We can never see anything in isolation, an object is always related to the one next to, in front, behind, on top or below it. Relations are important." (Dujardin-Beaumetz H., *op. cit.*, 1913, p. 36).

active feelings of sympathy …

STRATEGIC

"What struck me, on that day, was his air of meditation, the immobility of his pale face, his penetrating look, his silence. While his partners talked animatedly, laughed and gesticulated, Rodin seemed to be isolated from this tumult by his immense and thick beard, and smiling discreetly at their comments, remained impassive and silent." [1]

Charles Aubry,
RODIN WEARING A TOP HAT,
Printing-out paper, 1862, Ph.3.

"Paris is a strange city. It is enough to attach a little chime to a reputation for everyone to start ringing the bells. […] Thank heavens, Rodin did not have to wait for his consecration […] and in fact, within a fairly short period he almost became fashionable. Very fine writers hitched up to his chariot of glory" [2].

In 1881, the large-scale bronze of *Saint John* stood next to the *Creation of Man* at the Salon [3]. And all of Paris started to talk about Rodin. The controversy over *The Age of Bronze* that had erupted in 1877 established the reputation of the sculptor. Strangely enough, the doors of political and literary salons opened their doors at the same time as those of galleries for the sculptor who had just received the commission for the big *Gates* for the future Decorative Arts Museum from the State, and who had been pushed by scandals to the front of the artistic stage [4]. He was reputed to be slightly rebellious and solitary. And in fact this is what made him the centre of attraction. His reputation as an innovator was intriguing at a time when sculpture had come to an aesthetic standstill and started to be weighed down by inertia. "When Rodin appeared, sculpture was no longer of great interest to us" [5], confessed Geffroy in 1900.

Twenty years earlier, when Rodin moved into Rue Lebrun, he had apparently tried to reach out to the world. He was poor and was trying desperately to make himself known. He contacted the Société Nationale des Beaux-Arts through its Director, Louis Martinet. This society included artists as famous as Ingres, Delacroix, Baudry and Carpeaux, and exhibited the works of young artists in return for membership fees. Rodin took along his *Bust of Father Eymard* to a preview dinner as a sign of "his right to sit down with the mighty men whose presence he was now to enter.

LEFT PAGE

Anonymous,
RODIN AT THE RACES WITH HENRI ROCHEFORT,
gelatin silver print, 1900, Ph.703.

Rudolf Bruner-Dvorak,
BANQUET GIVEN IN HONOUR OF RODIN IN PRAGUE, 30 MAY 1902,
gelatin silver print, Ph.715.

Anonymous,
WANDA LANDOWSKA PLAYING THE HARPSICHORD IN RODIN'S VILLA IN MEUDON, 27 MARCH 1908,
gelatin silver print, Ph.1066.

PROGRAMME OF THE LITERARY AND MUSICAL ORGANISED IN HONOUR OF RODIN
by Mme Catulle-Mendès, at the Ritz,
28 June 1910.

Maurice Fenaille,
RODIN AT THE VISIT BY RAYMOND POINCARÉ TO MONTAL, AT MAURICE FENAILLE'S HOME, 13 SEPTEMBER 1913,
gelatin silver print, Ph.868.

1 Rodin at the preview of the Salon in 1988, quoted by Lecomte G., "Rodin tel que je l'ai vu", *Chefs-d'oeuvre de Rodin*, Paris, Publications Techniques et Artistiques, 1946, p. 7.

2 Bergerat E., *Souvenirs d'un enfant de Paris,* 3rd vol, Paris, Eugène Fasquelle, 1912, p. 253.

3 Now called *Adam.*

4 In 1882, Rodin took part in four exhibitions.

5 Geffroy G., "L'Exposition Rodin. Renaissance par Rodin", *L'Écho de la Semaine,* 10 June 1900.

[…] To his great comfort it was much admired, and he felt, for the first time in his life, that there was a ray of light not unwilling to fall upon his head."[6] The club was unfortunately dissolved shortly afterwards. However, there was enough time for him to meet eminent personalities, such as Théophile Gautier, about who he would say: "I met him once […] and with the confidence begotten of a glass of champagne, I tackled him in conversation. But I fear I said some stupid things, and that he did not pay much attention to my youth".[7]

83 - Juliette Adam,
INVITATION CARD TO RODIN,
1909, Ma.1151.

We are now far from the period when Rodin sought fame. Every Wednesday, Juliette Adam, a staunch republican and founder of *la Nouvelle Revue* in 1879, hosted one of the most influential salons of the Third Republic, where many political and literary personalities crossed each other's paths. Republicans would meet here, in particular the eminent Léon Gambetta. During the lifetime of Edmond Adam, the guests included Henri Rochefort, a journalist, critic, polemist and founder of *L'Intransigeant*, a scandal sheet, as well as Ernest Waldeck-Rousseau, who was still the Minister of the Interior[8], who showed an interest in Rodin in 1884 while he was working on *The Burghers of Calais*. It was also in the home of "the charming, enthusiastic and generous Mme Juliette Adam" that he was introduced to "Castagnary, a critic who was intelligently sensitive to Beauty, and later became the Director of Fine Arts. Although, in general, official artistic circles tended to treat me badly, and although the public, corrupted by so many banal works that were tumultuously glorified, paid no attention to my works, it was in this environment that I found active feelings of sympathy."[9]

Rodin did not hide himself. He would attend this Salon even more often when, at a certain point, it was frequented by rightist intellectuals and opponents of Dreyfus [10] … The correspondence sent by Juliette Adam to Rodin is much more prolific from 1906 onwards. However, "the political nature of Mme Adam in no way prevented the arts and letters from finding the most generous hospitality in her home. She gave place of honour to discussions that attracted an elite, and were organised freely and without affectation" [11], wrote Mauclair in 1909. So let us not predict anything.

6 Bartlett T.H., *op. cit.*, 19 January 1889, p. 30.

7 Lawton F., *op. cit.*, 1906, p. 171.

8 He was President of the Council from 1899 to 1902.

9 Lecomte G., *op. cit.*, 1946, pp. 11-12. Eugène Spüller, at the State Educational Department in 1887, had Castagnary as Director of the Fine Arts. He himself frequently visited Rodin.

10 "In her magazine *Parole française à l'étranger* (1900-1906), [Juliette Adam] would develop theories more or less based on facts but increasingly reactionary, anti-socialist, war-mongering and anti-Semitic." (Martinez R.-M., *Rodin et la politique*, a Master's thesis in art history, University of Paris X, Nanterre, 1988-1989).

11 Mauclair C., "Les salons littéraires à Paris", *La Revue des Revues*, 1st January 1909, p. 77.

12 Bazire to Rodin, s.d., Ma. 2465, Rodin Museum.

13 See Rodin A., *op. it.*, 1911, pp. 179-180.

14 See Rodin to Aline Ménard-Dorian, 13 May 1883, L. 335, Rodin Museum.

It was apparently Edmond Bazire, encountered after an article he had written, who introduced Rodin into this circle: "We will now meet at Madame Adam's, and your introduction into this home will be an excellent thing"[12] *(fig. 83)*. He introduced Rodin to many eminent personalities, including the great Victor Hugo, of course, but also Gustave Geffroy, a friend of Clemenceau and Rochefort, for whom he made a bust[13]. He was also responsible for his being invited to join the circle of Aline Ménard-Dorian, more or less at the same time as that of Juliette Adam[14]. The mansion in Rue de la Faisanderie, where Madam Ménard Dorian held her salons, was a meeting place for radicals and anti-clerics, and at the time of the affair, those who were pro-Dreyfus and leftists. The leading light at this salon was Clemenceau. Rodin would only meet him personally a few years later *(fig. 84)*, at a date that is still uncertain. Among the

84 - Auguste Rodin,
CLEMENCEAU,
terracotta, 1911-1913, S.741.

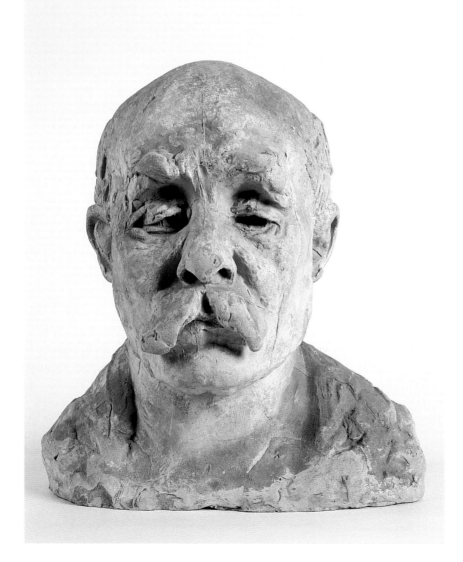

guests was Gustave Geffroy, who was soon highly considered and esteemed by the sculptor.

The latter was forty-three years old. He established the kind of political relations that would help him in his career and at the same time also frequented artistic and literary circles. Madame Liouville, the daughter of the famous Doctor Charcot, organised dinners on Saturday evenings [15]. This is where he probably came across Antonin Proust, at the very end of 1883. Other guests included Dalou, Monet, Mallarmé and Maupassant.

His friend, the engraver Félix Bracquemond, took him to see the writer Léon Cladel, who also received writers, artists, musicians and journalists at his house in Sèvres on Saturdays. Rodin would "arrive with a timid, almost gauche, air, that hid his courage." Rodin was considered to be a "curious chap" in these circles of artists and writers [16]. The most fiery and expressive pens from the press were found in these breeding grounds for ideas, in these melting pots of reflection and discussion. Those who had the means of propelling Rodin forward were there, and he had opportunities to forge indestructible friendships. Among them was the painter Eugène Carrière, recognisable for his "misty ideal" [17], whose portrait of Rodin would be used for the big poster of his personal exhibition in 1900. Avant-garde writers would meet at the Café Voltaire on Monday evenings. Rodin would join them whenever he felt like it. Some of his literary friends would soon pass away. Léon Cladel died in 1892, Guy de Maupassant in 1893, and the following year, Stevenson, with whom Rodin shared a fleeting friendship.

It is clear that Rodin had become a socialite even though he denied it [18]. "Rodin saw more society during these decade than either before or since"[19], according to Lawton. Much later, Cheruy, his former secretary, would come to the sculptor's defence: "Not that he was a society man, even then; he attended the dinners then because he was starving". And he quoted Rose Beuret to back what he said: "When Monsieur Rodin had to attend a dinner, I had to dry his only boiled shirt in front of the stove: I ironed his silk hat too. And as he could not go out with worn heels, I repaired them with bits of leather. If any bronzes were sold through those social acquaintances, the money was soon engulfed by the expenses for the 'Porte de l'Enfer'." [20]

[15] Although it is tempting to look for a possible source of influence, with respect to the tension that stretches bodies into an arch in Rodin's works, his attendance of Charcot's sessions on hysteria at the Salpétrière hospital cannot, unfortunately, be proved by any archive source.

[16] Cladel J., *op. cit.*, 1903, p. 19.

[17] Apollinaire G., *Chroniques d'art*, Paris, Gallimard, 1981, p. 306.

[18] "I have no taste for luxury, society and fine dinners. My comfort is my work and it is enough to satisfy me. I want my peace and quiet – time for myself, no quarrels." (Grunfeld F.V., *op. cit.*, 1988, p. 305).

[19] Lawton F., *op. cit.*, 1906, p. 72.

[20] Cheruy R., *op. cit.*, 20 January 1929.

In addition to these circles and salons, Rodin was drawn into a series of dinners and banquets held by groups, societies or reviews such as *La Plume*, to the famous banquets organised to defend the freedom of art, for which Rodin had gradually become a symbol. "To drink to Rodin […] is to drink to a young, personal, free and very lively art!"[21] In the same spirit, a number of spontaneous literary and artistic meetings took place. These included the dinners of the "Bons Cosaques" on the first Friday of the month[22]; the dinners of the "Pris de Rhum" where guests clearly enjoyed taking a stance against the Institute; the "dîners de la banlieue" organised by the painter Raffaelli; and those of the "Têtes de Bois" or the "Types Épatants". Rodin is known to have attended them at an early stage since the first reports of his presence in the press date to the early 1880s. Little by little, politicians who were aware of, and interested in, this aesthetic renewal came to these gatherings, a fact that sometimes put Rodin in a awkward position, especially at the time of the Dreyfus affair, for he was always careful about what people might eventually people say …[23]

But Rodin was already caught up in the system. He was solicited from all sides to support one cause or another, to preside over this or that meeting, or to attend sumptuous banquets for several hundred guests in honour of famous artists and writers *(fig. 85)*, for instance, the painter Puvis de Chavannes, Goncourt or his friend Stéphane Mallarmé, whose literary Tuesdays he attended. This was the price to pay for fame. But the efforts were well worth the useful relations he made through these circles, and they also led to recommendations and press coverage that brought him out of anonymity and pushed him to the centre of the stage.

His circle of relations had broadened considerably by the end of the eventful decade 1880-1890, which marked the start of his rise to fame. However, being true to himself, he had difficulty in playing the role imposed on him. As Francis Jourdain recalled: "When Rodin came to dinner at my father's place, he did not take part in the atmosphere created by his cordial and generous passion, nor did he get involved in any of the discussions. His impassiveness and silence aroused a feeling of awe in me. The attention that surrounded him seemed to embarrass him. Yet he looked neither anxious nor weary. He did not show anything. His shyness was obvious and I used to ask myself why on earth he accepted invitations that obviously gave him no pleasure."[24] Rodin would probably have answered with the words heard by the guests

85 - **Place-card at the banquet held for Victor Hugo on his 81st birthday at the Hôtel Continental, 27 February 1883.**

[21] Speech by Roger Ballu at a dinner given in honour of Rodin for his nomination as Chevalier of the Légion d'Honneur, on 21 January 1888 (quoted in *Paris*, 27 January 1888).

[22] "That is where I met Maupassant, seductive and capricious; Mallarmé, charming and incomprehensible […]. In that distant past, there were only fiery defenders among the young intellectual elite. Since then, many of them have abandoned me." (Rodin, quoted by Marcelle Adam, "Henry Becque et Rodin", *Le Figaro*, 22 May 1908).

[23] An exchange of letters with the Swiss poet and journalist Matthias Morhardt about invitations to the banquet to celebrate the seventieth birthday of Puvis de Chavannes in 1895, kept at the B.P.U. of Geneva, shows the infinite precautions taken by the sculptor.

[24] Jourdain F., *Rodin*, Lausanne, Jean Marguerat, 1949, p. 12.

at the banquet hosted by *La Plume* on 9 December 1893: "Unfortunately, I am only a simple manipulator of a chisel, and just as sculpture is silent, I have the right, if not the duty, to keep quiet." Since he realised that his name was guaranteed to attract funds, he willingly accepted the numerous requests from various juries, subscriptions [25] *(fig. 86)*, charities, and shows for charitable causes [26]. Rodin was therefore seen at concerts (he even organised them sometimes), at the theatre, which he hated, or wherever else he was expected to be. Occasionally but rarely, he refused, but it was always with a sense of guilt. He had the feeling that one day his absence would be to his detriment, as for example, the "invitation to a public dinner which I refused being tired and desirous of escaping further fatigue" [27]. He felt this refusal was responsible for the bad reception of his *Monument to Claude Lorrain*.

Inevitably, celebrity attracted not only socialites but also flatterers and snobs. After Edmond de Goncourt died in 1896, Rodin met Comte Robert de Montesquiou who introduced him to the circle of fashionable aesthetes, among them, Anna de Nouailles, for whom he would make a bust *(fig. 87)*, and to the salons of Comtesse de Greffuhle and Madam Arman de Caillavet. Up to 1900, it was in such circles that he finished

86 - Claude Monet to Auguste Rodin, **LETTER CONCERNING THE SUBSCRIPTION FOR THE OLYMPIA BY MANET,** 4 February 1890, Ma.2601.

25 Approached by Monet on 25 October 1889 for the purchase of the *Olympia* by Manet for the Louvre, he replied: "Put me down for 25 francs. It is just to include my name. I am short of money and cannot afford more." (Rodin to Monet, [late October 1889], location unknown).

26 All this was well before the war, during which such requests would multiply.

27 Lawton F., *op. cit.*, 1906, p. 145.

87 - Auguste Rodin, **ANNA DE NOAILLES,** terracotta, 1906, S.1090.

88 - E. Servant, **VISIT BY THE SCANDINAVIAN DELEGATION TO RODIN'S STUDIO,** 29 Novembre 1904, printing-out paper, Ph.779.

perfecting his image, even though he felt ill at ease. As the exhibition at the Place de l'Alma, on the fringe of the Universal Exhibition, attracted visitors of all nationalities, it finally turned him into a public man. Helene von Hindenburg and Isadora Duncan were but the most durable relationships that the sculptor forged in the white pavilion.

The addresses of all these people were carefully kept by his secretaries in numerous directories, sometimes grouped by country of origin in big notebooks, with a diagonal label or writing in violet coloured ink indicating the contents. The expansion of the Rodin "network" required careful organisation, well before 1900. The names included

89 - Auguste Rodin,
THE DUC DE ROHAN,
bronze, 1909, S.782.

those of leading European personalities and official delegates *(fig. 88)*, Prince Eugene of Sweden and the King of England, Edward VII, the Duc de Rohan *(fig. 89)* and the Princesse de Polignac, members of French high society and rich Americans who ordered their busts [28] *(fig. 90)*, a host of potential buyers, the Curie couple introduced by Loïe Fuller, and many others who have since been forgotten by history [29]. Some of them, like the rich industrialist Maurice Fenaille, who made a substantial contribution to spreading the sculptor's fame [30], became his friends.

A consequence of the controversy over the *Balzac* in 1898 was that Rodin's fame became international. Foreign journalists assailed him. Foreign artistic societies started to show an interest in him. The painter Whistler, for whom he made a funerary monument, arranged to have his work exhibited in London at the International Society. Bertha Zuckerkandl, a relative of Clemenceau, put him in contact with the Viennese Secession, while his first exhibition was held in Belgium and the Netherlands in 1899. Rodin was nearly sixty years old. Thanks to these exhibitions, he started to travel, in turn establishing new foreign relations that his fame attracted. The studio at the Marble Depository [31] was open to visitors on "Saturday afternoons", as indicated in English on the calling card of the sculptor of 182 Rue de l'Université. After 1900, visitors came to Meudon in greater numbers, probably because the Villa des Brillants was a more accurate reflection of the man who had sought refuge there, as well as his sculpture. As a crucible for Rodin's work, Meudon housed his studio, which had become almost like company, with about fifty people, most of them housed on the spot, assisting him permanently.

Rodin himself was the excuse for a banquet for 120 guest, held on 11 June 1900. Receptions given in his honour multiplied. His trips to foreign countries aroused ovations. His visit to Prague in 1902 was a triumph. He was now solicited as a prominent thinker, his opinion brought credit and his intervention aroused interest. With the exception of politics, a topic on which he refused to express himself all his life, he took part in all kinds of debates, starting with explanations of his own work, which newspapers thoroughly enjoyed.

28 For instance, Kate Simpson and Mrs. Potter Palmer.

29 "What a disappointing life I have ended up living, if I were vain I would like it. But I feel an antipathy for it because pure friendship, which I value so much, no longer exists in my home cluttered with clients, if I may say so. […] I am worn out by this unreasonable life that is so incompatible with my strength." (Rodin to Helene de Nostitz, [Paris or Meudon, 11 July 1909], L. 834, Rodin Museum.

30 He published at his own expense 142 drawings from the black period, heliographed by the Goupil firm and published by Boussod, Manzi, Joyant, in July 1897 (see *Figures d'Ombres*, Bordeaux exhibition catalogue, Goupil Museum, 10 May-10 August 1996, Bordeaux, Somogy-Goupil Museum, 1996.

31 "The Marble Depository – marbles intended for sculptors with State commissions – was composed basically of a very vast courtyard where, between enormous blocks scattered on the thick grass, monstrous geometric figures brought from quarries in Greece, the Pyrenees and Italy, grow graceful and simple grasses and wild flowers; […] Constructions made of planks and plaster tiles of a uniform model, with a continuous line, and a raised ceiling, windows wide open to the northern light, are allocated as studios to sculptors. A black letter on a white door marks out the territory of each one." (Maillard L., *op. cit.*, 1899, p. 22-23). "Rodin was formerly at M. he has now been given H to rough-hew his stones" (Riotor L., "Caractères et projets", *Rodin*, La Plume, special issue, V° fascicule, 1900, p. 74).

It was at this point that Claire de Choiseul entered the scene, shortly before 1907. The last infatuation of Rodin, this sparkling and compulsive forty-year old, who claimed to be a Duchess, set about winning the confidence of the ageing sculptor who was probably not very lucid about her intrigues. She made the prices of his works shoot up *(fig. 91)*. His friends started to worry: "She wants to dress up this artist, who is so simple and nice in his intelligent and thoughtful aspect as a manipulator of clay, as an elegant man of the world. She has had his thick bushy beard trimmed, waved and brilliantined, and turned the short, rough style of his hair into a high quiff, prolonged by a heavy grey chignon on the nape of his neck. He has given up wearing his ceremonious frock coat and suits from La Belle Jardinière, and only dresses in clothes made by the best tailors. She is gay and amuses him with her pranks and jokes. She is always calm and collected, showing great interest in all his different kinds of his work. […] this lady gives him a taste for all kinds of puerile vanities"[32], recalled Georges Lecomte. As for the faithful Rilke, he tried to reassure himself in 1909: "Perhaps Rodin really needs, at this stage, someone who is prudent, a little childish, who can help him climb down from the lofty heights he is constantly taken to. Once upon a time, he remained up there, and God alone knows how, where and through what night he ended up by returning. To see him now, so different from his usual self, one felt a little frightened for him; and unpleasant though it was for me, I understood the Marchioness who put on increasingly stupid records to finally fall on some popular dance tune"[33]. And yet he wrote this reminder, found among his papers, shortly before 1912: "Stop receiving D. in the afternoons because I am working"[34].

Little by little, made aware by those close to him of the abuse of confidence by the so-called duchess, he broke off with a heavy heart, paralysed with remorse for those close to him[35]. In the summer of that year, he confided to a journalist: "All that constitutes luxury, like parties and charming companions, no longer interests me. I am old."[36] And so Rodin was able to devote himself heart and soul to a plan that would use up his remaining strength: to create a museum bearing his name, and to retire finally to his villa in Meudon to work just for himself.

32 Lecomte G., *op. cit.*, 1946, p. 25.

33 Rilke R.M., Letter to Clara Rilke, Paris, 3 November 1909, *op. cit.*, Paris, *Le Seuil*, 1976, p. 144.

34 Notes and Drafts, III-A-6, Rodin Museum.

35 "And I had my wife, my poor little wild flower who I almost crushed, I had your friendship, all this time attracted by your youth …" (Cladel J., *op. cit.*, 1936, p. 291).

36 Rodin, quoted by Acremant A., Rodin écrivain", *Excelsior*, 27 December 1910.

above all controversies …

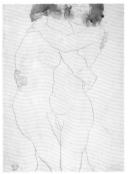

SCANDALOUS

"He arrived, worried and nervous. His face no longer had that serenity drawn from fruitful efforts; his forehead was furrowed with tenacious wrinkles, his expression, set among features easily inflamed by impatience or fatigue, wavered between eyelids reddened by the impact of thoughts which, when he gave instructions to his assistants, made his usually steady and clear voice abrupt. With an involuntary movement, his broad shoulders seemed to throw off an invisible burden. One felt that this normally placid mind was torn and eaten away by worries." [1]

François Antoine Vizzavona,
RODIN LEANING ON THE BUST OF NAPOLEON (DETAIL),
printing-out paper, 1910, Ph.858.

92 - Gaudenzio Marconi,
AUGUSTE NEYT, MODEL OF THE AGE OF BRONZE,
albumen print, 1877, Ph.272.

93 - Gaudenzio Marconi,
THE AGE OF BRONZE, PLASTER,
albumen paper, 1877, Ph.271.

"I was led to glory by paths I did not know - and I was only required to show just a little resistance and patience" [2]. In fact, the sculptor's repeated failures to be accepted by the artistic coterie would have discouraged many. It is a widely acknowledged fact that the first known figure by Rodin, the one on which he placed so many hopes - subsequently dashed - set off a public scandal when Rodin decided to submit it to the Salon. But this disappointment turned out to be a cloud with a silver lining for it drew attention on the sculptor who had spent nearly six years waiting in the wings in Belgium, while sculpting pleasant busts for a well-to-do clientele. His *Age of Bronze* affirmed his position, he had devoted more than one year's work on it, and was finally ready to exhibit at the Salon in 1877. The verdict was severe. Rodin was accused of deception: "it is said that I made the cast of a corpse and then stood it on its feet" [3], he wrote to Rose, who had remained in Brussels. Rodin appealed to the President of the Jury, in a letter written in April 1877: "Imagine that I had used my savings to work on a figure I hoped would have the same success in Paris as it did in Brussels, since the modelling seems to be well done and it is only the procedures that is attacked. What distress to see my figure, which could help me in a future that is taking long to come, for I am 36 years old, what distress to see it rejected by a withering suspicion." [4] Confident in the power of truth and deeply hurt, Rodin defended himself with all the energy of despair. Casts and photographs served as evidence *(figs. 92 and 93)*.

LEFT PAGE

RODIN REMOVING HIS BALZAC AFTER THE ALMA EXHIBITION,
La Presse, 27 February 1901.

Auguste Rodin,
BALZAC
terracotta on a wooden stand, circa 1897,
S.263.

Auguste Rodin,
SAPPHIC COUPLE STANDING,
graphite and watercolour on buff paper,
D.1543.

PORTRAIT OF RODIN,
Le Cri de Paris,
30 April 1905.

[1] At the time of the *Balzac* affair, in Cladel J., *op. cit.*, 1903, p. 44.

[2] Notebook n° 50, f°35 v°, around 1906 ? Rodin Museum.

[3] Rodin to Rose Beuret, [Paris, after 13 April 1877], L. 10, Rodin Museum.

[4] Letter to the President of the Jury of the Beaux-Arts exhibition, Mr. de Chennevières or Mr. Guillaume, [Paris, April 1877], L. 256, Rodin Museum.

94 - Auguste Rodin,
SAINT JOHN THE BAPTIST AND THE WALKING MAN IN THE HÔTEL BIRON,
bronze, circa 1880 and 1907,
S.999 and S.998.

For *The Age of Bronze* was both his destroyed *Bacchante* and the fruit of his encounter with Michelangelo. The contours were still too realistic because, as Rodin would explain much later, his main concern was to "render the admirable architecture of man's body" in a "very accurate reproduction". However, Rodin would soon overcome this concern for truth, which still produced "a certain coldness"[5] because it was too close to the profiles of the model. But for the moment, his concern for accuracy caught him in a trap and his indisputable talent as a modeller did him a disservice[6].

Rodin's honour was finally saved when a few friends, including several sculptors who were very much in the limelight, defended him. However, this inopportune adventure would set the tone to his career. Firm positions were the outcome of his successive failures to be admitted to the Salon. He stopped suffering in silence, and took action instead. "It's over, the State, sculptors and myself, we will never agree!"[7] He reversed the situation to justify his failures. Being an unyielding person, he would never let anything pass any more. Furthermore, he refused to accept the right of the State to make a mistake. He had invested too much in sculpture to be able to tolerate injustice.

Fortunately for him, the successive Secretaries of State responsible for the Fine Arts each had a different approach. The State purchased *The Age of Bronze*, and *The Gates of Hell* offered him an ideal theme to study the nude while avoiding confusion. "I had no idea of interpreting Dante, though I was glad to accept the *Inferno* as a starting point, because I wished to do something in small, nude figures. I had been accused of using casts from nature in the execution of my work, and I made the 'St. John' to

5 Cladel J., *op. cit.,* 1903, p. 39.

6 For details about *The Age of Bronze* and Rodin's stay in Belgium, see *Vers l'Age d'airain, Rodin en Belgique,* exhibition catalogue, Rodin Museum, 18 March-15 June 1997, Paris, Rodin Museum Publications, 1997.

7 Coquiot G., *op. cit.,* 1917, p. 101.

8 Bartlett T.H., *op. cit.,* 11 May 1889, p. 223.

refute this, but it only partially succeeded. To prove completely that I could model from life as well as other sculptors, I determined, simple as I was, to make the sculpture on the door of figures smaller than life, my sole idea is simply one of colour and effect." [8] He therefore started work on the *Gates* with a need to justify himself, to a certain extent. The scandal had turned *The Age of Bronze* into a manifesto and set in motion the sculptor's radical commitment to works that implied surpassing himself. *Saint John the Baptist, The Walking Man (fig. 94), The Burghers of Calais* and *Balzac* were the milestones along this road.

95 - Anonymous,
Rodin behind The Kiss in his studio at the Marble Depository,
printing-out paper, Ph.1221.

But for the moment, he was busy pursuing his research on the expression of passions that the theme of the *Gates* made possible. Paolo and Francesca stepped down from them in 1886 to acquire their autonomy, reunited in *The Kiss,* which today seems to be completely innocuous *(fig. 95).* As the French State commissioned a marble version of *The Kiss* two years later, Rodin hoped to use this group to temper the reaction to his *Balzac,* which he anticipated would arouse a stormy controversy when presented at his first exhibition at the Salon in 1898 *(fig. 96).* "Much criticism is levelled against me. I do not think I will be understood immediately …[…]. I do not have confidence in the public, given the objections already raised by my friends." [9] But it was all in vain. In that year, the two works marked his development over twelve years within the same space, and the sculptor needed to explain himself. "*[The Kiss]* is a big trinket sculpted according to the usual formula and which focuses attention on the two figures represented instead of opening up wide horizons to reverie. My *Balzac,* on the contrary, through its pose and expression, can make the imagination conjure up the environment around him, where he walks, where he lives and where he thinks. He is not separated from what surrounds him. He is like real living beings. In fact, the same is true of my *Walking Man.* He is interesting not for himself but because of the thought of the stage he has just crossed and the next one he will have to pass. This art, which deliberately goes beyond the sculpted figure to bind it, by means of suggestion, to a whole that the imagination gradually recomposes, is, I believe, a fertile innovation." [10] Nine years later, Rodin was still talking about it.

If he did not stop his explanations, it is because he realised to what an extent he and his critics did not speak the same language. The Société des Gens de Lettres, which had commissioned the work, was weary of having waited seven years for such a result, and being aware of its political impact in the midst of the Dreyfus affair [11], it rejected the statue. The press unleashed a series of caricatures, satires and violent indictments. The public wavered between outrage and amusement. Rodin was deeply hurt but he was forced to face the facts. His work on the transition, the edge, the border and interval between space and time, all the things that had increasingly helped him to capture movement, feelings and life in his sculpture, the entire abstract dimension of his research, was not noticed. Or not yet, History would say. From *The Age of Bronze* to *Balzac,* from strict conformity to the model to the full maturity of his work, too much in keeping with expectations, or not enough, Rodin was not a man of half measures, and even less of concession. Apart from the outrage caused by these two works that set the boundaries of his research, both the public and critics were disconcerted by the unfinished aspect of his works, as well as his audacity and scorn for conformity and official rules. In 1905, Adolphe Lambert criticised him in the

96 - Anonymous,
THE PUBLIC IN FRONT OF THE MONUMENT TO BALZAC AT THE SALON OF 1898,
printing-out paper, 30 May 1898, Ph.267.

9 Jeanès J.E.S., *op. cit.,* 1946, pp. 142-143.

10 Gsell P., "Propos d'Auguste Rodin sur l'art et les artistes", *La Revue,* 1st November 1907, p. 106.

11 It was Émile Zola, author of the famous "J'Accuse", published in *L'Aurore* of 13 January 1898, who had ordered the statue from Rodin in 1891 in his capacity as President of the Société des Gens de Lettres.

press: "When will this artist, so powerfully talented, understand that a plastic work does not exist by intentions but by clear thinking and precise forms, and that what really counts is that it is finished!" [12] And yet, as Rodin acknowledged, "I did not dare for a long time to implement all the ideas I had. I was always afraid to provoke a scandal. Now I am free of these apprehensions. I have only to follow my path." [13] But he said this in 1910 when he was seventy years old.

The great landmarks of his work, *The Burghers of Calais,* commissioned in 1885 to commemorate the sacrifice of the heroes of the town, and the *Monument to Victor Hugo,* both crystallised his new research by raising the assemblage to the rank of a monument. These works too did not receive the reaction Rodin hoped for. "This monument of the *Burghers of Calais*? […] I worked eleven years to obtain the right to make it in the way I had conceived it, based on a moving account by Froissart, a contemporary of the heroic men… They themselves were the contemporaries of the great Gothic cathedrals, which as you know I have always admired" [14].

LEFT PAGE

98 - Auguste Rodin,
THE BURGHERS OF CALAIS,
plaster, 1889, S.153.

97 - William Elborne,
**RODIN AND THE BURGHERS OF CALAIS
IN HIS STUDIO
AT 117 BOULEVARD DE VAUGIRARD,**
albumen print, circa 1887, Ph.6390.

The project was dear to his heart. In addition to the expression of suffering, Rodin sought to achieve immanence: "Eustache stiffens. He is the one who will talk. And he does not want his voice to tremble. He is immobile, but he will walk … This is something I thought a lot about …" [15], he told Jeanès. The contract was signed on 25 January 1885, and working in the very new studio in Rue de Vaugirard, he modelled the *Burghers* in clay - a technical feat - life-size and naked, according to his habit *(fig. 97).* There were six of them, Rodin wanted a group of figures, like a rosary of suffering, according to the sculptor's own words [16]. He also studied the rhythms of the concordance between the six big figures and the empty spaces. It was the first time he tackled this particular problem. The whole group had to be expressive and the public was invited to share its suffering, through the negation of a pedestal *(fig. 98).* The city would have liked to see the heroic dimension highlighted, but this was relegated to second place. A classical pedestal was inflicted on the *Burghers,* in Calais in 1895, and the monument was placed near "a public convenience" [17].

12 Lambert A., *Triboulet,* 30 April 1905.

13 Rodin, quoted by Acremant A., *op. cit.,* 27 December 1910.

14 Rodin, quoted by Lecomte G., *op. cit.,* 1946, p. 15.

15 Jeanès J.E.S., *op. cit.,* 1946, p. 132.

16 Rodin A., *op. cit.,* 1911, p. 114. Rodin was violently opposed to the standard pyramid-shaped composition. "I am directly opposed to this principle, […] which gives works […] coldness and a lack of movement, convention […] The cube gives expression, the cone is the horse, the pet subject of students competing for the Prix de Rome" (Rodin to Omer Dewavrin [August 1885]; municipal archives, Calais).

17 Coquiot G., *op. cit.,* 1917, p. 106.

RIGHT PAGE

99 - Eduard Steichen,
THE OPEN SKY, 11 P.M., BALZAC,
bio-chromate gum on platinotype,
1908, Ph.233.

More than the scandal that broke out in Weimar in 1906 over his drawings, described as "nauseating"[18], more than the discussions over the eroticism of his works and a reputation as a "great faun" that would follow him until his death, these defeats, shook the very foundation of his work and were therefore a cruel blow to him. He soon stopped trying to convince, and took up the *Balzac* as his torch: "This work which was laughed at, which people took the trouble to scorn because it could not be destroyed, is the outcome of my entire life, the very linchpin of my aesthetics. The day I conceived it, I became another man. My development was radical; I had renewed ties between lost traditions and my own period, which became tighter every day. Some may laugh at this declaration. I am used to it and am not afraid of irony. I therefore affirm very clearly that for me, the *Balzac* was a moving point of departure, and it is because its action is not restricted to myself, and because it is a teaching and an axiom in itself, that people are still fighting over it and will continue to do so for a long time. The battle continues, it must continue. As for the public, it cannot be blamed. The fault lies with its educators. The sense of beauty and taste for reason have been lost […] For me, knowing that life is short and the task enormous, I allow things to take their course and I continue my work, above all controversies."[19]

In 1898, he thought he could temper the consequences of exhibiting the *Balzac* with *The Kiss*. Two years later, he understood. He still exhibited *The Kiss*, isolated, within the framework of the ten-yearly exhibition, in the company of Mercié, Barrias, Injalbert and others. A little further away, in the dissident pavilion, the plaster *Balzac,* standing nearly 3 metres high in the axis of the entrance, dominated the display of the biggest part of his oeuvre, "above all controversies", like a lighthouse. A story without words, like an ultimate message sent to the public.

Balzac then returned permanently to the silence of Meudon. Rodin only authorised its image to be circulated through photographs taken in the moonlight in 1908 by the American Steichen *(fig. 99)*. "Your photographs will make the world understand my Balzac".[20] This was one final attempt to have it accepted.

[18] This would in fact be responsible for the resignation of Count Kessler, organiser of the exhibition.

[19] "Le 'Balzac' de Rodin", *Le Matin,* 13 July 1908.

[20] Eduard J. Steichen, text dictated to Grace Meyer, New York, MOMA, ESA; see Pinet H., "Il est là, toujours, comme un fantôme"; 1898. *Le Balzac de Rodin,* exhibition catalogue, Paris, 13 June-13 september 1998, Rodin Museum Publications, 1998, p. 199.

they will listen to him in the end …

OFFICIAL

"A white silk scarf entwined about his long fair hair that was gray, and his stream-like beard enwrapped him up to the ears. His old re-ironed top-hat, with eight high-lights' seemed like a shoot growing from his highly polished boots that were just visible above his snow-shoes".[1]

Albert Harlingue,
RODIN AT THE FUNERAL OF GENERAL BRUN, 27 FEBRUARY 1911 (DETAIL),
gelatin silver print, Ph.740.

"Universal suffrage! It would be excellent if it were really personal. Unfortunately, it is a shameful corruption, a monstrous traffic; voters are paid, or else they decide for those who offer them a "drink"; it is the flock of this or that party, and the ballot paper of these "sheep" will have the same value as mine, for example! […] Each deputy then acts not towards a general goal but for a particular interest; all of them, separately, look after a small number instead of taking the majority of the French into consideration; and then the little pieces are put together, modelled and polished by a clumsy management, and the total forms a failed work!"[2]

In 1907, the condition of the working class suffered from a crisis. The shortage of jobs generated social upheavals lasting for three years. The repression by Clemenceau completed the break up of the leftist union. The period was a very difficult one and Rodin felt very pessimistic. Looking upon the worker as "an unskilled labourer with no interest in his work, […] entertains himself by going to a bar […], a human machine who only works through habit and force, instead of producing because of an inclination"[3], he who was now at the height of his glory, described work as a saving grace. And if he wanted to leave his *Tower of Labour (fig. 100)* as a legacy[4] it was because he was convinced that only good could possibly come out of it. Runaway industrialisation and the general impoverishment of taste saddened the artist who was nostalgic about the days when "workers were called 'artisans', that is to say, they were 'artists' because there is no big or small 'art', there is only one *art*."[5]. Far from anti-democratic considerations, he censured the bourgeoisie, holding it responsible, and above it, the State: "the bourgeoisie is in favour and hinders the resurrection of France – Béranger once said that he had aimed arrows in the royal velvet doublets. I will aim arrows at the bottoms of the bourgeois"[6]. But these notes were never disclosed.

LEFT PAGE

Anonymous,
THE DEFENCE OR THE CALL TO ARMS,
albumen print, Ph.1320.

RODIN'S VOTING CARD FOR THE ELECTIONS OF 27 APRIL 1902.

MENU FOR A LUNCHEON AT THE ELYSÉE, 20 JUNE 1894,
(4 days before the assassination of Sadi Carnot).

Albert Harlingue,
RODIN AT THE INAUGURATION OF THE MONUMENT TO VICTOR HUGO AT THE PALAIS ROYAL, 30 September 1909,
gelatin silver print, Ph.10378.

100 - Auguste Rodin,
THE TOWER OF LABOUR,
plaster, 1898-1899, S.169.

[1] Blanche J.-E., *Portraits of a Life-Time*, London, 1937, p. 114 ; cf. Grunfeld, *op. cit.*, 1988, p. 505.

[2] Rodin, quoted by Duranteau F., "L'appauvrissement du goût français", *Le Gaulois*, 15 April 1907.

[3] *idem.*

[4] "Let them consider me as dead, leaving the tower of labour as my legacy, and like Alexander bequeathing it to the most worthy for his achievement, I thought like the Goth(ics) of raising a fine monument to labour, a minor divinity but a god nevertheless" (Notes and Drafts, IIIDb, Rodin Museum). Armand Dayot offered Rodin to direct the project in 1898.

[5] Rodin, quoted by Duranteau F., *op. cit.*, 15 April 1907.

[6] Notes and Drafts, IIIDh, Rodin Museum.

111

In reality, Rodin, who was at the peak of his glory, did not want to become involved. He was completely mistrustful of politics and even displayed a certain degree of disdain towards it. His behaviour, at the very least opportunist, was particularly ambiguous at the time of the Dreyfus affair, and the controversy over his *Balzac*[7] was eventually entangled with it. "[…] all he could do was to hesitate between defending a fine thought and maintaining a fine clientele"[8]. Lucien Descaves went even further when he published a virulent letter on the first page of *L'Aurore* on 1st June 1898: "So, it's true, Rodin, you are afraid of being *compromised*, classified, enlisted by signatures that are, alas, the same on your subscription lists as on the protests in favour of Zola! […] Rodin, you grieve us; Rodin, your precautions are as bitter as ashes!" His failure to take a position in an affair that divided France into two was very eloquent. Everything in his attitude urged him to be cautious and carefully avoid anything that could do him a disservice. Discretion is the better part of valour.

On the other hand, whenever it was a question of art, nothing could hold him back. Only the interest of his works preoccupied him. Denouncing the deterioration of taste and the aesthetic clichés of official art was a pretext to justify his position on the fringe[9]. This started in the year 1857 when his desire to enter the Beaux-Arts was thwarted: "[…] it was the Institute that ran the École des Beaux-Arts, judging the competitions, correcting the students in turn during one month. They condemned everything that recalled 18th century art, and those who, even remotely, claimed their roots from it were treated as heretics. I was unaware of this at the time; I only knew about it much later."[10]

Finally, he brandished this failure like an unexpected stroke of luck at not having to admit defeat through official art: "A stroke of luck indeed" he wrote simply[11] between two parentheses, like an ultimate appreciation. And there is no question that it was indeed luck because his difficult career path finally led him to glory, thus permitting him to claim that quality as an artist-artisan, outside official movements. By attracting attention to himself, he was undoubtedly able to reverse influences. However, Rodin was not yet aware of this. Like all artists of his time he needed the State. The sacrosanct Salon des Artistes Français continued to be a prerequisite for achieving recognition. Its conservative jury was composed of members of the Academy and the École des Beaux-Arts. Its verdict was irrevocable.

7 For details about the *Balzac*, see *1898, Le Balzac de Rodin*, exhibition catalogue, Paris, Rodin Museum Publications, 1998.

8 Dervaux A., *Notules parisiennes"*, *Arts et Lettres*, February 1906, p. 122.

9 "[…] there is a formidable education of taste that comes from academies, official temples, citadels of art, where the old classical spirit entrenches itself, deformed by the doctors of law! The art professions – decorative art, industrial art – are collapsing in distress, pathos and imprecision. Artists are produced according to the formula." (Rodin A., "Glanes du Matin", *La Gazette de France*, 21 March 1908).

10 Dujardin-Beaumetz H., *op. cit.*, 1913, p. 112.

11 Notes to Gaston Schéfer, Institute Library, Paris.

12 Gsell P., *op. cit.*, 1st May 1906, p. 100.

So in that year, in 1865, Rodin took the plunge and dared finally to present the mask of his *Man with the Broken Nose (fig. 101)*. A first attempt and a first rejection, triggering off a long series of disillusions. Forty years later, when describing it in detail, his rebellious tone spoke volumes about his bitterness: "To tell you the truth, I never subjugated my work to any School formula. Right from the start, I rejected the yoke of official art. What anger I provoked! The pundits of the Institute started by turning down my mask at the Salon, *The Man with the Broken Nose*, and this injustice was all the more painful in that my daily bread depended on the success of my efforts in those years. They then stupidly accused me of having cast my *Age of Bronze* from life, and they only accepted it with great reluctance. You will recall the furious attacks I suffered from at that time. They pursued me relentlessly with their inane and sarcastic remarks. They inspired all the objections put forward by the official commissions called upon to judge my works. They set up the spirit of the Institute against me, when I presented my *Claude Gellée*, which resulted in a battle over its erection in Nancy, my *Burghers of Calais*, mounted on a horrible pedestal against my wishes, and my *Balzac*, which was quite simply rejected. Every time I borrowed a genuine gesture from Nature, the Institute called it a hoax or an indecency. I would have succumbed if I did not have my inflexible determination and the passionate approval of independent critics to support me. It was a struggle that had worn out others before me: Rude, Barye, Carpeaux. The Institute argued fiercely over the commissions that they needed in order to survive. It delayed delivery of orders; it was the executioner of these great men; they came close to killing them! But I will not allow myself to be trampled. I even believe that if my example bears fruit, official art will not have much longer to live. Its fall will finally mark the emancipation of our school, which for one long century has been diverted away from Nature and subjected to pretentious and meaningless formulas." [12] Gsell, who listened to these remarks, added: "In saying these words, he raised his clear eyes, which flashed with pride and disdain." But despite everything he said, Rodin was ready to make concessions to win recognition and acquire the means to survive. He submitted Bibi's head again ten years later, this time cut in marble and with a fine band around the head in the antique tradition *(fig. 102)*. *The Man with the Broken Nose* was accepted. Rodin had learned his lesson.

But we have not come to this point yet. During the IIIrd Republic, many monuments dedicated to the heroes and great men of France were erected in the streets of Paris. Rodin took advantage of his situation by submitting models of Diderot, Rousseau and Carnot successively, but without success. Then came the monument in memory of the defenders of the Capital during the siege laid by the Prussians in 1871. Rodin modelled *The Call to Arms*, perhaps remembering that two years earlier, "in the Dome

101 - Auguste Rodin,
MASK OF THE MAN WITH THE BROKEN NOSE,
bronze, 1903? S.496.

102 - Auguste Rodin,
BUST OF THE MAN WITH THE BROKEN NOSE,
marble, 1874-1875, S.974.

of Florence, I contemplated the *Pietà* by Michelangelo with a deep emotion. This masterpiece, usually in the shadow, was at that moment lit up by a big silver candlestick. A young choirboy, of a perfect beauty, approached the candlestick, which was as high as he was, pulled it towards his mouth and blew the flame out. I could no longer see the marvellous sculpture. And this child seemed to personify the spirit of Death extinguishing Life. I kept this strong and precious image in my heart." [13] He endowed the wailing figure with the features of Rose. It was yet another failure.

He only managed to obtain one commission, and even that was fraught with difficulty. This was for a statue of the philosopher, d'Alembert, for the façade of the City Hall of Paris. At the beginning of 1880, Rodin was still unknown [14]. However, he did not have much longer to wait. His *Age of Bronze* would soon bring him fame. By the time proof had been provided of his honesty, nearly three years had passed. Edmond Turquet, who was full of admiration for Rodin, found in him the perfect artist to establish his mandate as Under Secretary of Fine Arts on an image of artistic competence and courage [15]. Rodin wrote to him on 1st January 1880, while he was waiting for his integrity to be cleared in the affair over the *Age of Bronze;* "I have been waiting for a liberal minister to take over these duties and to render justice to me. I did not know, being so engrossed in my work, that what I was hoping for was so near at hand. [16]"

In 1880, the State purchased the *Age of Bronze.* And in the course of the same year, Jules Ferry, Minister of Public Education and Fine Arts, signed the commission for *The Gates of Hell,* established by Turquet. "The French government intended to build a Museum of 'Decorative Arts' and my door was to be the entrance. The commission came at the right moment. The idea already in my head. The conception of the Gate really goes back to my first trip to Italy in 1875. In Florence, I saw the doors by Ghiberti and I studied Michelangelo. […] I read its history and was enthralled by the doings of these men of the 15th century. And then I read Dante, his "Divina Comedia". I always had it in my pocket. At every spare moment I read it. In fact, I had started a group of Ugolino before I saw M. Turquet. My head was like an egg ready to hatch. Mr. Turquet broke the shell." [17] Rodin was allocated a studio in the Marble Depository in Rue de l'Université *(fig. 103).* His career was launched, and with it his fame.

[13] Rodin A., *op. cit.*, 1911, p. 285.

[14] "Employed at the National Manufacture of Sèvres and having obtained an honourable distinction at the Salon this year, I have the honour to ask from your enlightened kindness a figure for the works at the City Hall. If a figure cannot be given to me, I would nevertheless be grateful to be entrusted with a bas-relief of decorative grotesque masks, etc, or another element of statuary that is sometimes an accessory to ornamental motifs." (Letter to the President of the Municipal Commission on Fine Arts for the works at the City Hall [Paris, around 20 June 1879], L. 919, Rodin Museum).

[15] "My compliments on your nomination as Grand Officer. This proves once again that I have not made a mistake in placing at the Luxembourg your statue, which was accused of having been cast from life, by placing Saint John the Baptist there and commissioning your famous Gate." (Turquet to Rodin, 20 May 1910, Ma. 2568, Rodin Museum).

[16] Rodin to Edmond Turquet, 13 January 1880, F21/4338, National Archives, Paris.

[17] Cheruy R., *op. cit.*, 20 January 1929.

103 - Anonymous,
**THE COURTYARD OF THE MARBLE
DEPOSITORY, RUE DE L'UNIVERSITÉ,
CIRCA 1900,**
The Marble Depository by Léon Montarlot,
Le Monde Illustré,
2 March 1901.

Despite his denials, he had become an official artist, a "national sculptor"[18], even though the State preferred to acquire his works rather than to order them. Only about ten commissions came after the *Gates,* including *the Kiss* in 1888 and, the following year, the *Monument to Victor Hugo,* intended for the Pantheon which had lost its function as a church in 1885. Nearly half of them were never honoured.[19] The gap separating Rodin's work from the expectations of his sponsors led to delays and postponed deliveries. The sculptor was perceived as being capricious, and the press thrived on such incidents.

Was Rodin privileged? There is no doubt about it. From 1880 until he organised his exhibition at the Place de l'Alma in 1900, he attracted all kinds of privileges. To start with, he obtained a second studio at the Marble Depository – an unusual privilege – which he occupied until his death. Then the State gave him considerable financial support, and even though the *Gates* swallowed up the money in real time, over 25,000 francs had already been paid for a work that was never delivered [20] *(fig. 104, following page).* And yet the State continued to pay without ever asking for accounts or sending reminders. The message was clear and many were jealous.

18 Alexandre A., *Le Journal des Artistes,* 23 September 1888.

19 Rodin was probably referring to this in a card to Y. Rambaud, on the subject of an article that was to be written by Mellerio: "above all, I do not want my Gates or the Victor Hugo to be discussed. This has become an old refrain that upsets me." [1897-1898], L. 1503, Rodin Museum).

20 The balance of 4,300 francs was paid a few months before he died, bringing the amount for the *Gates* to almost 30,000 francs, the equivalent of the purchasing price of the Villa des Brillants at an auction in 1895 (27,300 francs).

This jealousy was fanned by the fact that these honours were gradually followed by visits and requests from leading European personalities, and regular invitations from the Elysée. Rodin was soon invited to all official ceremonies and he was bestowed with all kinds of decorations and honours: the title of Chevalier of the Légion d'Honneur in 1887, honorary degrees from several European universities, and Officer of the Légion d'Honneur in 1892. He still managed to retain a sense of humour: "Ah! Now I am higher than Jean-Paul [Laurens], who is only a Commander. This time I cannot ask him to serve as my sponsor. It is against the regulations. I will have to turn to someone else". [21] He was later elevated to the rank of Grand Officer, on 16 May 1910. His natural unsociability had the upper hand: "The very day when, in 1910, fashionable Parisian circles gathered to celebrate his elevation to the dignity of Grand Officer of the Légion d'Honneur, when he was on the point of leaving his villa in Meudon, when he started to receive countless congratulatory telegrams from eminent artistic and political personalities all over the world, Rodin, who felt irritated and nervous by the concern over his appearance and having to write the message of thanks he wished to convey to the organisers of the banquet given in his honour, suddenly put his elbows on the table, placing his white head between his hands, and in front of me, murmured in despair, 'My God, my God, I am the unhappiest of men!" [22] , reported his secretary.

In ten years, Rodin's reputation was made; he needed less time to reach the heights of glory, which would be international in scope. Countries as distant as Argentina commissioned a monument from him at the turn of the century, and Japan showed interest in his work. And yet he remained deeply attached to his country, even though, it is true, it took a long time to recognise him. His reply to the commission for *The Burghers of Calais* was eloquent: "Do not fear of incurring a useless expense because it is rare to have such a wonderful idea and opportunity to arouse patriotism and abnegation", he wrote to the Mayor of Calais on 25 November 1884[23].

Years later, *The Thinker* would be brought down from *The Gates of Hell* to be offered to the people of Paris, by subscription, in a monumental version. "[…] I never intended to represent the highly intellectual man, the virtuoso of thought. My idea was to represent the man as the symbol of humanity, the tough, hard-working man who thinks who stops in the mid stof his labor to reflect on things, to exercise faculty that distinguishes him from the brites." [24] When erected in front of the Pantheon *(fig. 105)*

LEFT PAGE

104 - Eugène Druet,
TOP PART OF THE GATES OF HELL,
gelatin silver print, Ph.396.

21 Rodin, quoted by P.G., "Décorations", *L'A.O.F.,* 5 August ? (the year is illegible). Cézanne, who he met at Monet's home with Clemenceau on 28 November 1894, confided in an over emotional way that he was particularly touched by the simplicity of Rodin: "He is not proud, Monsieur Rodin, he shook my hand! A decorated man!!!" (Geffroy G., *Monet, sa vie, son œuvre,* Paris, Macula, 1980, p. 326).

22 Meunier M., *op. cit.,* 21 September 1918.

23 Moreover, it appears that he was convinced of having arrived in time "to save the furniture" and was fully aware that his work would go down in history. An isolated and undated note confirms his involvement, far removed from any self-interest: "my goal is to make sculpture – this is not the same thing as working for commissions. It implies reinventing antique and authentic traditions. I work for the renown of France and am not making a profit out of all this, at my own risk". (Notes and Drafts, I, Rodin Museum).

24 Rodin A., " Every country has its beautiful women, says Rodin ", no reference.

105 - Marcel Hutin,
INAUGURATION OF THE THINKER
AT THE PANTHEON,
albumen print, 1906, Ph.754.

in 1906, it became, above all, the emblem of the power of liberal art: "*The Thinker* in front of the Pantheon is perfectly beautiful! […] An artist should not worry about being understood immediately. It is enough that he should understand himself, that is to say, not to accept anything contradictory in his mind. If his contemporaries do not understand immediately what is revealed to them, it is of no importance. They will eventually understand. For men are all made in the same way. And it is impossible for the strong emotions felt by one of them not to be shared by the others sooner or later." [25]. Rodin referred to his *Thinker* as a symbol of the equilibrium he was always capable of handling between his convictions and interest, his private life and career, his certainties and work, at the crossroads of his intellect and his hands. In other words, it was the perfect reflection of his image. It was significant that he achieved glory in the working-class district of the fifth arrondissement where he was born sixty-six years previously.

25 Gsell P., "Auguste Rodin", *La Revue de Paris,* 15 January 1918, pp. 405-413.

26 Rodin to Escudier, [end of 1909], L. 1264, Rodin Museum.

27 Cladel J., "The greatest French sculptor, the master Rodin, will be thrown out of the Hôtel Biron, which he had helped to save", *Le Matin,* 27 November 1911.

Half way between the people and the State, is it pure chance that the first statue by Rodin to be erected in Paris is *The Thinker* exhibited in front of the Pantheon, as if paving the way for making art more democratic, an idea that was dear to the sculptor? There was still a long way to go before arriving at the creation of his museum. But *The Thinker* was already a milestone in the ambitions Rodin had always nursed to be introduced to the people by the State.

He had occupied his rooms on the ground floor of the Hôtel Biron *(fig. 106)* for less than a year when the question was raised, during the summer of 1909, of selling the building and its garden at the end of the current year. As a result, Rodin came up for the first time with the idea of setting up a museum for his works. "I give the State all my works in plaster, marble, bronze and stone, as well as my drawings and collection of antiques that it was my great pleasure to assemble for the training and education of artists and workers. And I request the State to keep in the Hôtel Biron, which will be the Rodin Museum, all these collections, giving me the right to reside in it for the rest of my life." [26] Needless to say, the proposal was turned down but the sale was postponed. And gradually, the idea made progress. "A Rodin Museum must be created. This gift should be given to the Paris of work and reflection. And it must occur during the lifetime of the artist, who would quite naturally feel committed to leaving his works to his homeland" [27], wrote his friend Judith Cladel. This was only just the beginning of a long series of measures that would require much energy and influence to draw up an interminable list of signatures. And this despite the fact that the idea of giving Rodin the right to occupy the Hôtel Biron for the rest of his life aroused jealousy and rancour on which the press feasted, especially in 1912.

At long last, the successive donations of 1916 fulfilled the dream of the sculptor who was now reassured that his works would not be dispersed and could thus be offered to everyone. He had thought at length about the educational presentation of the Rodin Museum, which opened in 1919, two years after his death. He passed away in the middle of the war. There was a serious shortage of coal and the Villa des Brillants was icy cold. He died of pneumonia on 17 November 1917. Owing to the war, a solemn burial service was held at the last minute instead of the national ceremony announced in the press and planned for him as an ultimate tribute *(fig. 107)*.

106 - Cl. Lémery,
THE HÔTEL BIRON VIEWED FROM THE STREET,
gelatin silver print, circa 1912, Ph.9025.

NEXT DOUBLE PAGE

107 - Pierre Choumoff,
FUNERAL OF RODIN IN MEUDON,
gelatin silver print, November 1917, Ph. 1012.

I will not allow myself to be trampled …

OBSTINATE

"He moved forward with the heaviness of a massive elephant, tubby but elegant. His feet rose and fell in one block, with the solid slowness and the clinging, rhythmic lightness of the crushing feet of an elephant swaying from side to side. Even his bony face, tormented yet tranquil, showed traces of this fine animal in the rough, powerful and fine outline of the mass, the admirable patience, implacable obstinacy and tireless gentleness". [1]

Charles Hippolyte Aubry,
RODIN IN A SCULPTOR'S SMOCK,
gelatin silver print, circa 1862, Ph.4.

I t started with demands, those of a stubborn teenager who wanted to prove to his parents that La Petite École was the right choice. In 1854, Rodin was not yet aware of how difficult the path he had chosen would be. He plunged into a life of frenzied work, backed by his father, who did everything to ensure his success, without sparing his encouragement and assistance. The very first bust that has survived to these days, sculpted when he was twenty years old, was of his father, treated in an antique style, like a tribute [2]. He had no fear of work, in the sense of sacrifice. Solitary fulfilment was very much in keeping with his taciturn temperament. "Yes, I always loved work intensely. When I started, I was puny, extremely pale, the pallor of my poverty; but an ardent and nervous over-excitement pushed me to work without respite." [3] "Only the satisfaction of creating permits an artist to face difficulties, gives him a ruthless courage to sacrifice his interests and those of his family, and enables him to forget the sadness of yesterday, the fatigue of today and the worries of forever" [4], he admitted later, perhaps with a feeling of loss as a result of neglecting everything except sculpture. Those years were devoted, as he himself said, to "studying the technical part of my art, making my hands more supple. Before thinking of becoming an artist, ambition must be restricted to being a good craftsman." [5]

When he left the family apartment ten years later, he already claimed to be "an experienced modeller" [6]. In 1871, when he was on the point of leaving for Belgium, all that was left was to make progress by going beyond a perfectly mastered technique. "[…] if I had not been so stubborn, I would not have done what I achieved. The art of statuary is made up of strength, accuracy and determination.

LEFT PAGE

Emile Bergerat,
PORTRAIT OF RODIN,
albumen print, 1886, Ph.256.

Anonymous,
METAMORPHOSIS OF OVID,
albumen print, touched up with pencil by Rodin, as of 1886, Ph.343.

Auguste Rodin,
STUDIES FOR THE PEDESTAL OF THE BALZAC,
graphite on buff paper, after January 1897, D.7678.

[1] Meunier M., *op. cit.*, 21 September 1918.

[2] "Father was not pleased because I refused to do his side whiskers, which he wore like a magistrate … He could not accept that having sculpted it in antique style, I had to eliminate them." (Rodin, quoted by Tirel M., *op. cit.*, 1923, p. 68).

[3] Coquiot G., *op. cit.*, 1917, p. 25.

[4] Dujardin-Beaumetz H., *op. cit.*, 1913, p. 94.

[5] Fuss-Amore G., "Figures contemporaines vues de près. Une journée passée chez Rodin", *La Meuse,* 4 December 1903.

[6] Dujardin-Beaumetz H., *op. cit.*, 1913, p. 118.

108 - **AGREEMENT BETWEEN RODIN
AND VAN RASBOURGH,**
12 February 1873, Ma. 1065.

To express life, to render nature, you have to want to do it with all the strength of your heart and mind"[7]. When he returned to Paris six years later, he had changed, even in the way he perceived the artists he used to admire[8]. For him, Belgium always remained the "country I love like my open air studio, so to speak."[9] And for a very good reason too. But this new way of learning from nature required no less effort. As he himself summed up: "All my life has been a kind of study. My goal was never to have commissions but to study"[10]. However, "to study, you have to advance slowly, you must desert this century with its hectic life and resign yourself in advance to not making a fortune."[11] His friend Coquiot reported that "Rodin, ambushed in his studio, was like a frantic madman working relentlessly on his clay. All he knew about 'news from outside' were snatches of information reported by various people, or through those useful newspaper "headlines" that he could read distractedly. […] And what is the point of all this when the fate of a genuine artist - historically and traditionally - is to invent works despite the indifference of some and the imbecile jealousy of others!"[12] Rodin had subscribed to several press-cutting services as of 1880, and he received all the articles about him; he had some of them translated by specialised offices or his secretaries. His perception of the world was filtered through reactions to his work.

His only ambition was to search for a truth that he could make his own, far removed from the academic plasters and official education that were denied to him, and to prove that those years of youth were not sacrificed to sculpture but had enabled him to survive. The only thing that was important to him was his own perception, the only criticism he accepted was his own. In this respect he was intransigent.

The period when, as a good employee and assistant to Carrier-Belleuse, he was forbidden to sign any works produced by the studio, did not last long. This thankless job, carried out behind the scenes - others would do the same for him later - was rejected by Rodin in June 1871, when he decided to put his name on certain works exhibited in Antwerp. Did the probable dispute with Carrier-Belleuse over this decision lead to Rodin being dismissed? Or did Rodin leave on his own accord? In any event, he was soon burdened by severe financial difficulties[13]. In 1873, he signed a contract with another partner, Joseph Van Rasbourgh, to work together

7 Dujardin-Beaumetz H., *op. cit.*, 1913, p. 19.

8 "[…] when I came back to Paris my idols had fallen in the dust. I saw that we had no successors to Puget and that we were really going down hill. The statues I adored before I went away, I could not bear after I have returned. I do not like sculpture made from plaster casts, it has no life." (Bartlett T.H., *op. cit.*, 9 February 1889, p. 65).

9 Cheruy collection, University of Princeton library; cf. Grunfeld F.V., *op. cit.*, 1988, p. 82.

10 Rodin A., *op. cit.*, 15 March 1910, p. 207.

11 Rodin A., *op. cit.*, 1914, p. 68.

12 Coquiot G., *op. cit.*, 1917, pp. 96-100.

13 "Can you imagine, my little Rose, I have had many problems, I have not worked for nearly three months, which have been very hard for me, as you will understand. Monsieur Carrier and I had a dispute, however, things will work out, you will have to wait a little longer Rose, I do not have a penny at the moment". (Rodin to Rose Beuret, [Brussels, after 3 June and before 1st October 1871], L. 2, Rodin Museum).

Auguste Rodin,
LANDSCAPE IN BELGIUM ?
Red chalk drawing on buff paper,
between 1871 and 1877 ? D.7.

on various buildings in Belgium which, following the footsteps of Paris, wanted to have a face-lift (*fig. 108, previous page*).

Unfortunately, the partnership with Van Rasbourgh turned out to be shorter than planned: "[My employer] would come to the studio when I was absent – he did not dare to come when I was there – and oblige Van Rasbourgh to alter [my figures], to their great injury. I left them hardy and vigorous but Van Rasbourgh's changes, and the wretched way that they were executed in stone, have made them round heavy and lifeless. I was so disgusted with this that I lost all interest in the figures and never went near them while they were being cut." [14] The contract, originally intended to last twenty years, turned to the advantage of Van Rasbourgh and terminated itself four years later.

In the final analysis, Rodin could only work on his own. The few people he accepted in his work had to be subordinate to him. When he became famous, especially after 1900, many were busy at work in Meudon: marble cutters and sculptor's assistants, casters, studio workers and makers of plaster models. Some of them came to learn in the shadow of Rodin, to earn credibility for having frequented his studio. And they came in spite of his well known bursts of anger: "Sometimes, without any external warning sign, without any apparent reason, his expression would darken with a formidable excess of anger, followed by fierce and sudden mood swings. Without an outburst in his voice, without even a gesture, one would suddenly see, in the calm that precedes the outbreak of a storm, the face of the master becoming so scarlet that his red skin would show through the twists of his thick white beard." [15]

When it came to sculpture, Rodin made no concessions at all. Maratka, a young Czech sculptor, who had joined the studio in 1900 as an assistant, talked about "this other Rodin, the 'terrible Rodin' who terrorised everyone" [16] and who quarrelled with many of his assistants. For in Rodin's studio, the creation of the work and its execution were carried out in two stages. And his assistants had to bend to his demands, and even achieve the impossible, no matter how and at what cost.

As Bourdelle, his friend, put it: "He is […] terrible, Rodin. He said […] I did not take him seriously!", and he went on to relate the uncompromising comments of

14 Bartlett T.H., *op. cit.*, 26 January 1889, p. 45.

15 Meunier J., *op. cit.*, 21 September 1918.

16 Maratka J., *Vzpominky a Zaznamy*, (Notes and Memoirs), Prague, published by Odeon, 1987.

17 Bourdelle to an unknown person, 18 February 1902, unknown location ; see, Drouot-Rive Gauche sale, Paris, 21 and 23 March 1977, n° 40.

18 BBC Television, *Sir Gerald Kelly Remembers*, n° 4, "Rodin", p. 8 (X-23); cf. Grunfeld F.V., *Rodin*, Fayard, 1988, p. 616.

19 Rodin to Monet, Montrozier, 22 September 1897, location unknown ; see Geffroy G., *op. cit.*, 1980, p. 359.

the master: "I want a faithful copy of the mask - nothing more - I am the one who makes my compositions. I did not ask anyone to compose!!!" [17] Gerald Kelly also described "the master, a little dishevelled, and definitely irritable" supervising the assemblage of muses around the effigy of Victor Hugo for his monument - "I worked and swealed all through that morning while these women were moved out by these cranes", until he abruptly declared, "C'est affreux, changez tout. And so we swing these women about and we put them in other positions and during the whole of that day we moved them and I don't believe any progress was made." [18]

Even Claude Monet, only two days younger than Rodin - "my fellow traveller" [19] as Rodin called him - suffered the consequences of the sculptor's terrible character. A joint exhibition - "but only you and me" wrote Monet [20] - planned for 1889 in the luxurious Georges Petit gallery in Rue de Sèze *(fig. 109)*, finally left a bitter taste for both of them [21]. The Goncourt brothers wrote in their diary about how difficult to was to obtain concessions from Rodin who on that day placed his sculptures despite and to the detriment of Monet: "I don't care about Monet, I don't care about the world, I am only concerned with myself." [22] As for Monet, he replied: "I had trouble containing myself yesterday seeing Rodin's strange behaviour … All I want now is to go back to Giverny and find some peace." [23]

Galerie Georges Petit

8, RUE DE SÈZE, 8

Paris, 19 Juin 1889.

Messieurs **Claude Monet** *et* **A. Rodin** *vous prient de leur faire l'honneur d'assister à l'inauguration de leur Exposition, qui aura lieu le vendredi 21 juin 1889, de 2 heures à 6 heures,* **Galerie Georges Petit,** *8, rue de Sèze.*

De la part de M.

109 - **INVITATION CARD FOR THE INAUGURATION OF THE MONET-RODIN EXHIBITION, 21 JUNE 1889, AT THE GEORGES PETIT GALLERY IN PARIS.**

It is astonishing how naïve, and almost surprised, Rodin could be when he confided in 1915: "I don't know how I manage it, I quarrel with all my friends." [24] Was he in fact capable of understanding? Having an individualistic nature bordering on egoism, he was just as demanding on himself. Sculpture, being so deep-rooted in

[20] Monet to Rodin, Giverny by Vernon, 28 February 1889, Ma 2600, Rodin Museum.

[21] For details about the "Monet-Rodin" exhibition of 1889, see *Claude Monet-Auguste Rodin,* centenary of the 1889 Exhibition, exhibition catalogue, Paris, Rodin Museum Publications, 1989.

[22] "[…] it seems that some terrible scenes occurred, in which the mild Rodin, suddenly[brought out] a Rodin unknown to his friends (Goncourt E. and J. de, *Journal,* 23 June 1889, Paris, Robert Laffont, Bouquins Collection, volume 3, p. 285).

[23] Wildenstein D., *Monet, Vie et Œuvre,* volume III, Lausanne-Paris, 1979; cf. Grunfeld F.V., *op. cit.,* 1988, p. 310.

his case, came above everything else. His relations with others, non-existent outside the context of his sculpture, were inevitably connected with his work. No temperance was therefore possible, as the sculptor's assistants knew to their great expense.

Those who commissioned works from him came up against constant delays. "I am sometimes reproached for being excessively slow and demanding in the execution of my marbles. But I cannot consider them to be finished until I am completely satisfied. And I am difficult, especially on myself." [25] As for concessions, they were impossible to obtain: "[…] I will refuse absolutely to change anything whatsoever in the way they wish." [26]

From the multiple to the unique work, ordered and expected, there were many casts, and many alterations and hesitations that delayed or prevented full completion. Tirelessly productive, the search for suitable mouldings for his *Gates*, for example, lasted an entire lifetime *(figs. 110 and 111)*. He travelled specifically for this purpose, insatiably collecting architectural details from French monuments, which he endlessly recorded in his notebooks, while casts of architectural fragments piled up in Meudon. "I am becoming an architect", he wrote to Rose, "I must because in this way I will complete what is missing for my Gates" [27]. In 1904, he admitted to his secretary René Cheruy that he was not "satisfied with his architecture. I would like to work a little more on the moulding". Cheruy added that he wanted "to compose a moulding that would be precise enough to play the role of a frame for his composition but at the same time with a tone that would be soft enough to link it to the surrounding atmosphere." [28] Apart from the *Balzac,* finally accomplished, and the constantly studied cathedrals, there would not be enough time to apply the ultimate understanding of the lesson learned from Antiquity on the transition, the edge and the relationship of the work with its environment to *The Gates of Hell*: "Alas, the deadlines! There lies the problem! One should not *search,* go back on one's work, destroy things one considers to be bad, perfect others that seem, on the whole, to be absolutely finished. This, alas, is the story of my life. People have always felt that I did not arrive on time. It has been repeated for a long time that I was slow at work. Slow! During the works for the Exhibition of 1878, when I was employed by the ornamentalist Legrain, I would frequently model a life size figure in a few hours! But there you are, I have always muddled up dates; I have no notion of time when I am executing my work. Will I finish *this Gates* one day? It is quite

24 Cladel J., *op. cit.,* 1936, p. 318.

25 Rodin, quoted by Le Nain Jaune [G. d'Apremont), *L'Écho de Paris,* 15 March 1903.

26 Rodin on the subject of the *Balzac,* quoted in "Rodin et les gens de lettres", *La Cloche,* 12 May 1898, reprinted in *La Nation,* 13 May 1898.

27 Rodin to Rose Beuret, September 1890 ; cf. Cladel J., *op. cit.,* 1936, pp. 236-237.

28 Cheruy R., *op. cit.,* 20 January 1929.316 Coquiot G., *op. cit.,* 1917, p. 103.

29 Coquiot G. *op. cit.,* 1917, p.103

30 Rodin A., *op. cit.,* 15 March 1910, p. 210.

31 Letter by Alexandre Boucher to Rodin, 17 May 1910, Ma. 3567, Rodin Museum.

32 Gsell P., *op. cit.,* 1st May 1906, p. 97.

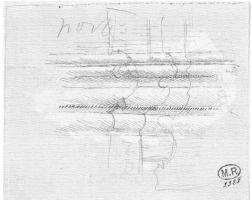

unlikely! And yet, all I need is a few months, perhaps two or three at the most, to finish it." [29]

With a similar intransigence, he pursued the truth of movement, the slightest manifestation of life, working after nature to achieve an accurate line, for nature did not accept imitations. His address books were covered with names of models who had approached him, with personal comments added next to them: "Giradot Vincent", for example, "very handsome like an antique, to take". Many presented themselves spontaneously at his studio. They were not necessarily professional models, far from it. And Rodin had no hesitation in taking his distance from them, detecting instantly the false tone of their School movement [30] in order to find the one who would serve his purpose perfectly. He therefore questioned his sculptor friends or took advantage of chance encounters, or he even went in search of the ideal model himself, especially for the commissions he received for monuments in honour of personalities who had passed away.

Rodin took pride in meeting the dead, and in fact he did meet them, and even anticipated them. One day, for instance, he accosted Alexandre Boucher, "the retired Director of Railways of Local Interest in the Landes" [31] on a train from Paris to Meudon, and asked him to pose so that he could finish the bust of the American Edward H. Harriman, who had died in September after three sitting sessions. The drawing artist Louis Malteste sat for the portrait of *Baudelaire*, to complement the photographic material in his possession, about which the sculptor, needless to say, insisted on asking preliminary and systematic questions. Estager, a carrier at Azay-le-Rideau, incarnated Balzac *(figs. 112 and 114)*. For Rodin, the real was sacred. "[…] to evoke this dead person, I drew inspiration from life. I was in the Touraine, the cradle of the great novelist. I selected several models who resembled him, and I made these busts of them, all summarised in a single one." [32] It was not a question of copying but of varying, of diverting, until he felt life springing forth, just as he

110 - Auguste Rodin,
MOULDINGS,
graphite and stump on a notebook page,
D.5527, notebook 3, fᵒ1 vᵒ.

111 - Auguste Rodin,
MOULDINGS OF A DOOR PILASTER,
annotated in graphite « door », graphite,
pen, ink and gouache on buff paper,
D.3328.

wanted it, precisely, for his *Balzac*, the one he would bring back to life. He set aside the tests, the busts that were simple copies, anything that was merely a semblance of life, and the imitation masks in which Balzac was still absent. If Rodin was anything, he was stubborn because during a period when portrait photographs served their purpose, he wanted to attain what was perhaps unattainable – resemblance – and to thwart all the traps of illusion and pretence into which so many of his contemporaries fell. Naturally, such unremitting efforts could not be understood, especially since the result fell so short of expectations.

The only way to bear such incomprehension, therefore, was to adopt an obstinate attitude, permanently. What critics took for excessive pride was undoubtedly the only means Rodin had at his disposal to justify his work and to continue it. He was sure of his position, he was sure of himself, and this is why he systematically ignored official opinions, of which he had formed his own views long ago. "I may have made mistakes with my *Balzac* as to certain details, but I believe in the truth of the principle by which I had conceived it, and expressed it in the way I felt. It is not commercial sculpture. [...] For *The Burghers of Calais,* for *Hugo,* for *The Gates of Dante,* for all my work, to the best of my ability, I reacted against tyrannical trends. I do not believe I was mistaken. But who will judge if not time? I have faith"[33]. "Against me I have all the unrelenting hostilities of the Institute. [...] I descend from cart drivers from Normandy; I am obstinate like the members of my race; I do not suffer unduly from the underhand traps laid out for me. I defend myself by standing firm. On my own, I have executed more works than all the sculptors of the Institute!"[34]

33 Ryp, "La question Rodin-Balzac", *La République Française*, 13 May 1898.

34 Coquiot G., *op. cit.*, 1917, p. 108.

RIGHT PAGE

112 - Anonymous,
ESTAGER, CARRIER FROM TOURS, MODEL FOR THE BALZAC,
albumen print, Ph.1217.

113 - Anonymous,
MASK OF BALZAC ON A COLUMN,
printing-out paper, retouched with ink by Rodin, Ph.1211.

114 - Anonymous,
THREE STUDIES FOR THE HEAD OF BALZAC,
albumen print, Ph.1213.

my college is life, teaching is love

PEDAGOGIC ?

"The master spoke with a slow and almost low voice while stroking his beard. His eyes, which are slightly red due to insomnia caused by continual cerebral tension, usually seem to be immersed in a dream. In fact, they are frequently lowered; but suddenly, when he stresses an idea, he raises them, and then his light blue look, which seem to come back from very far, darts at his interlocutor as if to penetrate him like an arrow."[1]

"I want to give you the principal, less small stories and more about what I think, because one only has value through ideas", Rodin told Gaston Schéfer briefly, in a few words, after the latter asked him in 1883 for some details with a view to writing his biography. It is true that Rodin was not a man of facts. It took him nearly forty years to make himself known, and twenty more to achieve fame, with his major exhibition of 1900. An entire life, not sacrificed but directed by and for his work, a life that he wanted to stand out as an example for young artists, just to be able to tell them: "It is possible".

He himself felt that he never had a teacher, and although the education he received was precious to him, it is probably because he was able to go beyond it and use the knowledge he acquired for his own purposes. Gustave Larroumet confirmed this in 1897: "Rodin did not have any masters and did not follow any schools. He is a worker who was elevated to art by the force of nature and the effort of work."[2] In keeping with what he had expressed in his youth when his mother enquired about the price to pay for artistic studies[3], he was a self-made artist.

Nothing much came out of the increasing requests from young sculptors to join his studio as students and even though Rodin dispensed advice, he hardly had enough time to devote to teaching. Yet many claimed this status, based merely on a word or an encouragement. It was a question of prestige. As Bourdelle confirmed: "I was not Rodin's student. He did not have any students, so to speak. He did not know how, he was unable to teach. I was one of his assistants. […] He would not give us any instructions other than a word from time to time: "More supple … More spirited … More human"[4]

1 Gsell P., *op. cit.*, 1st May 1906, p. 95.

2 Larroumet G., *Petits Portraits et Notes d'art*, Paris, Hachette, 1897, p. 225.

3 "I don't want any professors. I can work it through alone" (Bartlett T.H., *op. cit.*, 19 January 1889, p. 28).

4 Bourdelle, quoted by Bringuier P., "À propos d'une information américaine. Ce que Rodin doit à Bourdelle et ce que Bourdelle doit à Rodin", *Le Journal*, 18 March 1928.

115 - Albert Harlingue,
**JULES DESBOIS IN HIS STUDIO
NEAR THE BUST OF RODIN,**
gelatin silver print, Ph.13627.

In surrounding himself with assistants, he expected them to follow their own footsteps after having watched him at work. "The apprentice, the journeyman, the master, united in the same thought, devote a whole life of labour and effort to their task, these are the craftsmen of true art; the master working before his students, demonstrating the secrets of the craft as in the past, a constant example to follow, imitate, surpass."[5] Jules Desbois, a talented sculptor and friend of Rodin, worked in his studio as of 1884[6] *(fig. 115)*. He who had already exhibited at the Salon would confess many years later: "All that I know, I learned with him". Pompon, who became a great and well-known animal sculptor, joined him in 1890, his friend Bourdelle in 1893.

Rodin evidently knew how to surround himself with the right people. And these great and already talented artists were, in the end, more collaborators than assistants. Bourdelle is quite clear about the ambivalence he felt, from admiration to the struggle against being absorbed, from friendship to professional relations: "Despite my admiration for the master, I did not want to linger too long in his waters, invigorating though they may have been. An artist like him enhances his country and raises the dignity of humanity. His teaching, like his examples, is fertile. But a humble stream gains nothing by merging into the waters of a big river; it is swallowed up and gets lost. I have no intention of allowing myself to be swallowed up. The future will say whether I was wrong."[7] Rodin was invasive and tentacular. Bourdelle would go as far as to say: "I owe much to him, a lot of technique, but that is all. He killed, he killed all his students, all his disciples. I broke away from him in my art and he realised this five or six years before he died, and asked me, "Bourdelle why are you looking for something else?" And he got angry with me."[8]

By a strange irony of fate, it was with Bourdelle and Desbois that he envisaged setting up the Institute to which he would give his name at the beginning of 1900, "in competition with the official teaching of the École des Beaux-Arts", according to the press. Success, however, cannot be kept waiting. "It is up to you, master, to crown your great career by spreading your good word, all of Europe is already represented in your school"[9], Bourdelle wrote on 19 February 1900. Over thirty students had rushed to

5 "L'enseignement des beaux-arts: à propos du rapport Couyba. L'opinion de MM. Rodin, Besnard et Tronchet", *L'Éclair*, 23 December 1901.

6 He had met Rodin in 1878 at the ornamentalist Legrain, when he was working on the grotesque masks of the Palais du Trocadéro for 3 francs an hour.

7 Bourdelle, quoted by Thiébault-Sisson, "Au jour le jour. Nos artistes racontés par eux-mêmes", *Le Temps*, 4 August 1905.

8 Gimpel R., *Journal d'un collectionneur*, Paris, 1963, p. 95.

132 Boulevard Montparnasse to learn how to sculpt live models, a far cry from the lifeless academic plasters. But Rodin did not commit himself and never really came to the classes. Bourdelle tried again. "To remind you that if you have some spare time we hope to see you at the students' studio in Bd Montparnasse." [10] In the end, the adventure only lasted a few months.

For Rodin, theory was not constructive and the only lesson to learn was from oneself. He demanded hard work and great efforts: "*Teacher* is a word that no longer has any meaning, a hackneyed word. […] As a matter of fact, the best lesson that I can give is there: it is my work, let them observe it! The young and the intelligent will learn everything from it that can help them. Let them look and work!" [11] And so, rather than teaching, for which he barely had the time or inclination, he invited people to reflect on his sculptures and watch him work. Using the Universal Exhibition of 1900 as a pretext, he looked upon his pavilion in Place de l'Alma as a study centre: "In asking for this concession, I had but one goal: to exhibit the work that I carried out throughout my life, and not for advantages, as some of your colleagues have said. It will be a place for study, not for exploitation." [12]

At the end of the 1850s, when he presented himself for the competitive examination for admission to the École des Beaux-Arts, he already had an audience: "[…] during the minutes of rest, the students would gather round me, observe attentively [my study], tell me how highly they thought of it; they had no doubt that I would be admitted." [13] In any event, these were reasons to reassure him of his talent and capacity to transmit. But he would always refuse to do so, managing without words to explain pure technique.

On the other hand, at the bottom of his heart, he secretly hoped that his progress would be understood. Developing ideas, explaining forms, giving the keys to understanding to a difficult public, with a taste influenced by all and sundry at the academic school, gradually became a pressing need. The omnipresent press, not always indulgent, demanded explanations from him. Because his fame was the result of scandal, he obviously needed to justify himself; and because he did exactly as he pleased, despite the confidence shown in him by the State, he was obliged to defend himself.

Despite the fact that he was acclaimed in England and showered with ovations during his trip to Prague in 1902, Paris still had reservations about him. It is enough to recall

Eugène Druet,
RODIN AND PAUL CRUET IN THE STUDIO IN MEUDON (DETAIL),
printing-out paper, Ph.412.

9 Bourdelle to Rodin, s.d., Ma. 2566, Rodin Museum.

10 Bourdelle to Rodin, 5 March 1900, Ma. 2565, Rodin Museum.

11 Cladel J., *op. cit.,* 1903, pp. 25-26.

12 Rodin, quoted by an unknown person, " Le pavillon Rodin ", *La Revue artistique et industrielle,* April 1900.

13 Dujardin-Beaumetz H., *op. cit.,* 1913, p. 112.

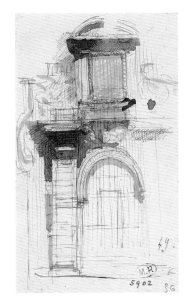

116 - Auguste Rodin,
PORTAL IN TOULOUSE,
pen and ink wash on buff paper,
August 1889 ?, D.5902.

118 - Auguste Rodin,
PROFILES OF MOULDINGS AND FACE,
graphite, pen and sepia ink on buff paper,
D.3450.

the words of Paul Leroi, published in 1903 in *L'Art;* "[…] this did not stop him, since his principal gift is that he is the craftiest of egoists, from duping the State and its dear taxpayers, in a way no artist has ever dared. […] this door is far from being finished but is an abundant source of income thanks to the use of numerous fragments constantly reproduced to be sold to the good Americans"[14]. That year, his defenders, Judith Cladel and Camille Mauclair among them, actively started to publish articles about him. It needed the monumental *Thinker,* offered to the people of Paris by subscription, the one placed in front of the Pantheon in 1906, to persuade people. As for Rodin, he needed time to explain himself.

Although he was very efficient in organising publicity for his work – the considerable press campaign centred on the exhibition at the Place de l'Alma is a perfect illustration – his first publications took a while to come out. He waited to be solicited, he excited the curiosity of journalists, but he himself said very little. He contented himself with replying to questions. A succession of interviews followed, and people flocked to him with requests. This was the price to pay for glory. The interviews were not always about his work and could centre, instead, on more frivolous, futile and interesting subjects. "He was sometimes accused of giving his opinion on many subjects, on too many subjects! But it was always his extreme courtesy that was responsible for his undoing! If you only knew how many people – men and women, French and Eskimo journalists, blue stockings and lovers of lust – would flock to the Hôtel Biron for the most ridiculous interviews, you would be quite aghast."[15]

In 1913, he finally decided to publish the results of his meditations in a book, under a title that came as no surprise, *Les Cathédrales de France.* This was the outcome of rewriting his profusion of intimate notes, which crystallised his need to discuss, to share the lesson from the Middle Ages and primeval nature that guided him all his life. It was published in 1914, just before the war broke out. Rodin used this architecture to base his arguments on ornaments, on how to channel observation, and on the savoir-faire of men. He drew from it all that was possible in terms of structure without stinting himself.

Soon Rodin would have one single goal: to transmit in order to avoid deviation. His notebooks and studies were an invaluable complement to his sculptures and drawings. "In my youth, I thought for a long time, like others, that the Gothic was bad; I only understood it when I travelled; my obstinate labour has not been useless, and like one of the wise old kings, I finally came to prostrate myself."[16] As Paul Gsell reveals, many

14 Leroi P., "Treizième exposition de la Société des beaux-arts", *L'Art,* April 1903, p. 232.

15 Coquiot G., *op. cit.,* 1917, p. 39.

16 Rodin A., *op. cit.,* 15 March 1910, pp. 215-216.

17 Gsell P., " Auguste Rodin", *La Revue de Paris,* 15 January 1918, pp. 410-411.

18 "Une lettre d'Auguste Rodin", *Les vandales en France,* special issue of *L'Art et les Artistes,* 1915, p. 16.

recall "having seen him at Notre Dame, immobile, standing against a pillar upon which he rested his temples. Unaware that he had been spotted, his day dreaming continued without being distracted by the faithful brushing past him. He was familiar with these raptures. They made his friends tremble when they accompanied him outside because when he was lost in his thoughts, he walked ahead without paying any attention to the congestion in the streets." [17]

Studying architecture became a passion and a perpetual lesson that grew over time from an attachment to ornaments and details to the extreme simplification of mouldings, work on structure, and abstraction *(figs. 116 and 117)*. For Rodin, architecture was an entire world of sensations that eventually overwhelmed him. "[…] at the end of a career of laborious activity and infinite ecstasy, I finally dwelled on our cathedrals and churches of France, in the cool shade bathed in the odours of the past, after a long and pious initiation into our medieval art, which alone […] was capable of attaining the supreme accomplishment of both architecture and sculpture." [18] In the twilight of his life, Rodin would add nature. When his work on pedestals emerged as the embryo of a reflection on this question, cathedrals, and through them, structure, the Gothic style and the human body echoed and joined each other *(fig. 118)*. The geometry Rodin developed as being unquestionably the only universal law governing equilibrium and movement, was part of a whole. [19]

This unique book, which on its own summarised Rodin, was published in time, on the eve of the war, as if it were an omen. And from then onwards, the conflict influenced the content of other messages for Rodin no longer held himself back. His resounding cries of alarm over the destruction of national heritage by the enemy were repeated in many newspapers and reflected his strong feelings about the restoration of churches, a few years earlier [20]: "[…] the German canon booms over there, and we must react to it. To its fire, we

117 - Auguste Rodin, **Notre-Dame Cathedral in Rodez,** ink and sepia ink on buff paper, August 1889 or 1897 ? D.3532.

19 "[…] my art proceeds from architecture like geometry. A body is a building and a polyhedron" (Mauclair C., "Notes sur la tecnique et le symbolisme de M. Auguste Rodin", *La Renaissance Latine"*, 15 May 1905, p. 206.

20 " I arrived in Rheims and it was very painful for me to see what has been done over the years to the cathedral, one of the jewels of the land of France. Here, a head is being remade, there an arm or leg is adjusted, and this is being done with no feelings for art, by merchants and not by artists. Why? Out of ignorance." (Rodin A., "Pour la défense des églises", *La Libre Parole,* 5 April 1911).

must retaliate by an even deadlier fire. […] We can have no other thoughts"[21], he wrote in *Le Journal* of 17 March 1916, in a final spurt of anger. Rodin spoke for France. He had become a symbol.

At long last, after the year 1900, people finally listened to him thanks to his fame, and the sculptor was able to base his credibility on comments about topics other than his own work. Now that he had support and had nourished himself with lengthy reflections, he was in a position to talk about peripheral subjects that gradually moved further away. This was a pretext to go beyond, or fall short of, the point in question. And when he finally sought to justify himself, he understood the power of dissemination and used it effectively. As a result, he was believed, erroneously, to be a great connoisseur of antiques. People came from everywhere to consult him. He cultivated his image. He took advantage of the situation to intensify his criticism of the Institute and official art, the bourgeoisie and restorers of buildings and open their eyes on the evocative powers of the forest, "the vegetal cathedral"[22], the lessons learned from Antiquity to the Renaissance, and the geometry of movement. In other words, he spoke and he wrote.

RIGHT PAGE

Anonymous,
Rodin installing The Clenched Hand and Imploring Figure,
gelatin silver print, 15 December 1906,
Ph.671.

In anticipation of the time when he would no longer be there, he concentrated on the creation of his museum. This would take up all the energy of his remaining years, like a journey back to his work. Along with the apprehension of death, came the unspeakable fear of not having finished, of an incomplete oeuvre, frozen in eternity. All that remained for him to do, therefore, was to assemble everything so that he could donate it to the cause of comprehension and organise his departure like a gigantic lesson, the only, posthumous and final one[23]. Since he had collected and kept everything that was part of his life in order to leave the keys to his work, his donation marked a final wish, a gift to see and think about[24]. With *Les Cathédrales de France* as the keystone, he also demonstrated the power of his sculpture and the lessons of the past. Transmitting "to preserve for our children the great lessons of this past that the present is unaware of"[25], to insert it as a link in the chain of history, and to continue talking about pleasure. "I too will die, but what ardour, what youth, this French architecture of bygone days has given me. […] But before disappearing, my studies will be rewarded, and if I have not been understood, I have enjoyed them, I had the good fortune of loving, which I can pass on to others".[26]

[21] Rodin A., "Pour chasser les barbares – Il faut utiliser toutes nos énergies", *Le Journal,* 17 March 1916.

[22] Meunier M., *op. cit.,* 15 April 1914.

[23] "[The State] can in this way create, without any financial inputs, an educational centre that I feel is profitable." (Rodin, quoted by Aubry R., "Rodin dans les jardins de l'Hôtel Biron", *Courrier de la Plata,* 13 May 1912).

[24] "In any event, I bequeath my work to the State; I have therefore more than paid my debts to it." (Coquiot G., *op. cit.,* 1917, p. 103).

[25] "Pour faire aimer les cathédrales: le grand sculpteur Rodin les explique", *Le Matin,* 29 October 1909.

[26] Notes and Drafts, IIIDb, Rodin Museum.

And so Rodin left everything to us. Gone are the cigar boxes in which he classified his papers in alphabetic order. Lost are the keys to furniture and rooms that held his secrets, which he kept "in a small leather pouch resembling that of a bank messenger, and always wore around his waist in Meudon"[1].

Can we trust the locks that he had put in his life? He had arranged everything in such a way as to ensure that he would be one single oeuvre in collective memory. A personality overtaken, almost ingested, by his titanic work. Although there is no doubt that he was misunderstood, he did not try to understand that such a life, pushed to the point of forgetting others, to the point of forgetting himself, was humanly unbearable. The man was divided between Meudon and Paris, like his works are today. Excessively protective, excessively revealing, he led a dual life that made him elusive from whichever side we stand on.

Rodin's extraordinary feat was that in disappearing, he had nevertheless organised himself to reverse the engines. As he had, in fact, done all his life, by turning his "failures into his own glory"[2]. By giving us, the public, his most personal notes, allowing us to have in hand the letters his mistresses asked him to destroy, and preserving the meaning of his heritage to the detriment, one last time, of the man himself, he left us more than we hoped for. In addition to his work, he finally consented, in an ultimate act, to mix his private and public life, his life as a man and as an artist, Rose and Camille, by relying on time to record his story.

He has never been so close to us. The paradox that confronts us is that during his lifetime, this man, who was extremely suspicious by nature, now summons us as witnesses to his life, even its most intimate aspects. It is as if, not having had enough time during his lifetime, he wanted to tell the world about the ascendancy of sculpture to which he gave everything and which, in turn, took everything from him. And in trying to understand this and mulling over it, captivated by the man and on the lookout for what he has finally given us, we again forget the main point, his raison d'être and the reason why we have been allowed to share the intimacy of his life: his countless, protean works.

"Rodin is dead, long life Rodin", one could almost acclaim casually, as if it were the only certainty remaining to us. But dare we venture further? He himself wrote: "I will have a narcissus cast in bronze, it will serve as my stamp"[3], like a secret, on a loose sheet of paper, in a final confession, a loop closed like Rodin over himself, or rather like Rodin over his sculpture. Because in the end, we inevitably return to the same point: Rodin at work.

---

[1] Gsell P., *op. cit.*, August 1923.   [2] Gsell P., *op. cit.*, 15 January 1918.   [3] Notes and Drafts, VIDe, Rodin Museum.

Faithful

The roots, fidelity and constancy of a life.
The people: family, friends, teachers and useful relations.
The places: the 5th arrondissement of Paris, Beauvais.
The centres of interest: reading.
The discoveries: botany, architecture and the 18th century.
The training: teachers and methods.

Avid

The need to learn in order to understand.
The capacity to absorb the visible and the need to accumulate and multiply for the purpose of moving ahead.
Taking notes.
Collecting forms through sketches, the sketches themselves, then objects.
Multiplication in parallel with his own works.
Understanding the whole through the detail, the mass through the component.

Independent

The capacity to move away from the masters to make progress, a slow digestion of the lessons learned, the first decisions to be free in his sculpture, and the first works.
From ornamentation in architecture, adding figures and movement, to *The Gates of Hell*.

Sensual

The pleasure and ability to enjoy life, the need for solitude.
The effects of pleasure on his work, personal life and relations.
His relationship with the visible, food and women.

Curious

The need to understand which guided his entire life, but experienced day by day in an irrational way.
First, the ancient masters: Michelangelo, the Middle Ages.
The new: exoticism.
The different: women.
The familiar: movement. An investigation of the signs of permanence in each new thing and a search for a universal law.

Secretive

What Rodin concealed for fear of hindering his career: Rose, his son.
His image: his suffering, his feelings.
His peace and comfort: his mistresses.

Bold

How the public perceived his personal work.
The audacity of undertaking research in the course of a work.
The view of the public compared to that of the artist.
The unfinished and the incomplete.

Strategic

Launching a career through decisive encounters.
Adopting a strategy: the decade 1880-1890 through literary and artistic circles,
Then 1890-1900 through fashionable circles, and after 1900 through visits and
social events.
The price of glory.

Scandalous

How his works were received.
The diagonal view of chronic misunderstanding.
Controversies as the landmarks of a career.
The positive impact of an artistic scandal.

Official

The relations between Rodin and the State, those that represented him and the one he
represented.
His lukewarm and overcautious positions.
The art of making the most of disparagement.
A permanent equilibrium.

Obstinate

Energy channelled into sculpture.
The means used to achieve fixed goals.
Intransigent in his work and, consequently, in relations with his assistants.
The difficult of self-questioning from a human point of view.

Pedagogic?

A determination to be understood.
A vocation to pass on the results of his research as a visionary.
From justifying a career built on incomprehension to didactic explanations.
Dissemination aimed at teaching how to observe.
The donation as the ultimate lesson.

ALREADY PUBLISHED BY THE RODIN MUSEUM

2003
Camille Claudel & Rodin, Time will heal everything

2002
Rodin, Antiquity is my Youth
Rodin, The gates of Hell
Rodin, Hell and paradise

2001
Rodin, The Burghers of Calais

1998
1898 : Le *Balzac* de Rodin
Rodin dans l'Allemagne de Guillaume II

1996
Rodin - Les marbres de la collection Thyssen
Rodin et la Hollande
Rodin à Meudon

1995
Monet en Norvège

1993
Le Salon de Photographie

1992
80 dessins de Rodin

1991
Camille Claudel

Diffusion : musée Rodin

Illustrations credits

© musée Rodin: cover, figs.1, 6-27, 29, 31-33, 35-38, 41, 42, 44, 45, 50-52, 54, and pages 22, 33, 42-43, 52-55, 67-68, 76-77, 88-89, 100-101, 110, 122-123, 132-133, 135, 139.
© musée Rodin: photo Adam Rzepka: figs.3-5, 10, 20, 21, 28, 30, 39, 40, 43, 46, 48, 55, 56, 61, 65, 70, 74, 75, 78, 84, 87, 89, 91, 94, 98, 100, 102 and pages 32, 42, 54, 76, 100, 125.
Photo Erik Hesmerg: figs. 76 and page 132. Photo Jérôme Manoukian: figs. 101.
Photo Jean de Calan: figs. 1, 115 and page 7, 140. Photo L. Joubert : fig. 34, 48 and page 54.
© musée Rodin and © Photo Bruno Jarret/adagp: page 42.

ISBN : 2901428819

French Version: 2901428800